TALES
for
TRAINERS

Tales for Coaching
Using Stories and Metaphors with Individuals & Small Groups

'I strongly recommend anyone who aspires to be an effective modern coach (or mentor) to read this book.'
—Eric Parlsoe, Author, *Coaching and Mentoring*

Demonstrating the most effective way of using stories when coaching individuals or groups, the book comes with 50 tales for a range of situations including: goal setting; problem solving; reframing and creativity; empowerment; success and self esteem.

Paperback 0 7494 3521 6

Tales for Change
Using Storytelling to Develop People and Organizations

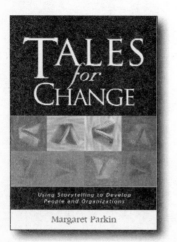

Frogs change into handsome princes, ugly ducklings into swans: traditional storytelling is rich in powerful images of change and transition. Using 50 stories to reframe business problems and provide useful metaphors for the boardroom, office and individual, this book is a powerful and innovative tool for making change happen.

Paperback 0 7494 4106 2

TALES *for* TRAINERS

Margaret Parkin

KOGAN
PAGE

London and Sterling, VA

First published in 1998

Reprinted 1998 (twice), 1999, 2000, 2002, 2004

Kogan Page Limited
120 Pentonville Road
London N1 9JN
UK

Stylus Publishing Inc.
22883 Quicksilver Drive
Sterling VA 20166-2012
USA

www.kogan-page.co.uk

British Library Cataloguing in Publication Data

A CIP record for this book is available from the British Library

ISBN 0 7494 2510 5

Typeset by Northern Phototypesetting Co Ltd, Bolton
Printed and bound in Great Britain by Clays Ltd, St Ives plc

Contents

Contents

Introduction

What's the story of *your* life? Maybe you're a newly appointed trainer, or manager with responsibility for training, who's looking for innovative ways to 'get the message across' and facilitate the learning process. Maybe you're an experienced trainer, wanting to 'spice' up your well-practised material. Or maybe you're a coach or lecturer, looking for new ways to bring things to life for your audience.

If you can relate to any or all of these situations – then this book is for you. The purpose of this book is to serve as a ready-made resource – a tool kit, carpet bag or jewel box, depending on your choice of metaphor – for trainers and educators to use in a variety of ways. The hope is that it will also make you more conscious of what personal stories and anecdotes you already use, and stimulate your interest to look for more.

Stories have always been used as a powerful tool for communicating vital information from one generation to another; they have always been used as a vehicle for the wise to educate the young. And we know that they are highly successful. If not, they would not have survived.

This book is divided into two parts. Part One gives you a brief overview of stories, metaphors and myths and the purpose they have played over the years – and still do today. It explains how and why stories help to facilitate the learning process, and gives guidance on where and when they might best be used in a modern business setting.

If you are the storyteller, there is advice offered on how to deliver the material, how to achieve and maintain rapport with your audience and how you can make the best use of your voice and body language.

Part Two is an anthology of 50 tales, wide-ranging in style and content. Some of them are in traditional fairy tale genre and might be hundreds of years old, some are personal anecdotes that happened last week. But the tales do have at least two things in common: they have all been used (in some cases, many times!) successfully with audiences, learning groups or individuals, and they all have potential and relevant learning in the form of a message or moral.

Although my feeling is that stories have most impact when read aloud or told to a group, they can also be powerful if listened to on tape, or even if used for personal reading. Stories adapt themselves wonderfully to fit in with individual learning styles! None of the stories in the anthology lasts more than around ten minutes if read aloud, and some are as short as 30 seconds.

It seems to be debatable as to whether you should divulge the intended message of a story, as different individuals can and do find their own meanings. Bearing this in mind, I have not been prescriptive in how the tales should be used, but I have given my own suggestions as to where I have found the message fits most appropriately in a learning context. Whoever is reading the story can then make the decision as to where a tale might be most useful and also whether to divulge the moral, or leave it to the audience to form their own interpretations.

I hope this book will illustrate that using storytelling to facilitate and make learning more pleasurable is not advocating any unfamiliar or fly-by-night practice, but merely returning stories, metaphors and myths to their original purpose and rightful place in our society.

PART ONE

The Story So Far...

CHAPTER 1

Once Upon a Time ...

STORYTELLING TRADITIONS

'Once upon a time ...' well how else could you possibly begin a book about storytelling other than with those immortal words? And now just stop and think for a moment how you felt when you read those words. Happy? Relaxed? Engrossed? Did you imagine them spoken in a particular person's voice, perhaps soft and lilting? Or did you have a sense of anticipation as to the pleasure that was to come?

If you felt any or all of those sensations, then don't worry; you're in good company! With very few exceptions, the love of hearing a story is universal. Stories transport us back to our (relatively!) carefree childhood days, when we were used to hearing stories, both at home and at school. Even those for whom school was regarded as a necessary evil, 'story time' still held a certain inexplicable magic.

The art of telling stories has always been an essential part of human nature. Stories, metaphors, myths and legends, together with their relatives – anecdotes, similes and analogies – have all been used as methods for communication and teaching since time began. They have travelled successfully from the early writings of Aristotle and the Greek myths and legends, the parables of Jesus, *Aesop's Fables* and the *Canterbury Tales*, through to *Gulliver's Travels*, *Grimm's Fairy Tales* and George Orwell's *Animal Farm*.

Telling stories is a uniquely human experience. Whereas animals can, to a limited degree, communicate their own personal experiences to each other, we human beings have developed the skill of abstraction, that is we are capable of communicating not just our own but others' experiences, with the purpose of providing access to a greater and more cumulative wisdom, the wisdom of our ancestors.

Of course this wisdom, although crucial for our personal and cultural development, might not always be pleasant. Storytelling does not always consist of 'roses round the cottage door' and '… happy ever afters'. One Eskimo storyteller said: 'Our tales are men's experiences, and the things one hears of are not always lovely things …'

In fact, some of the original fairy tales written by the likes of Grimm and Hans Christian Andersen were far too gruesome and shall we say 'colour-ful' to be told to children. For example, the romantic scene with which we are all so familiar of the handsome Prince waking Sleeping Beauty with a kiss is apparently only half the original truth. In the unabridged version, she was indeed woken up, but a kiss wasn't the only thing on the Prince's mind! These days, a scene like that would have to end in three dots …

It is only in relatively recent times that some stories, particularly fairy tales like the one mentioned above, have been edited and 'cleaned up', and subsequently become more associated with children. Although in most traditions it was indeed the old that educated the young through tales of their own and others' experiences, telling stories was by no means seen as a childish or trivial pastime as it is regarded by some today.

Indeed, Bruno Bettelheim, in his research on the subject, discovered that in traditional Hindu medicine, the prescription of a fairy tale was not uncommon in the treatment of an emotionally disturbed patient.

> It was expected that through contemplating the story the disturbed person would be led to visualise both the nature of the impasse in living from which he suffered, and the possibility of its resolution. From what a partic-ular tale implied about man's despair, hopes and methods of overcoming tribulations, the patient could discover not only a way out of his distress but also a way to find himself, as the hero of the story did.
>
> (Bettelheim, 1991)

Those who think that contemporary stories are simply the domain of chil-dren, should be reminded that the majority of books borrowed from libraries – by children *and* adults – are all stories of one sort or another. And any adult who is a regular viewer of the many 'soap operas' that now appear on our televisions should be reminded that their prime rea-son for tuning in religiously every night is simply to find out 'what hap-pens next' – the essence of every good story!

Before the printed word, storytelling existed in every nation throughout the world, and each had its own traditions: the Celtic culture had their Bards and Druids, the Norsemen of the Scandinavian countries told sagas, the Islamic countries listened to teaching from Sufi masters and dervishes while the people of Mongolia and Siberia were influenced by the tales and medicine of the shamans.

What all these tales had in common was that they captured the imagi-nation of their audiences in such a way that they were committed to memory; they were handed down from generation to generation and became part of that nation's culture. In many cases these stories still survive today.

And it's amazing to see how some stories have apparently travelled across time and continents – Coyote, who was originally a god in North-American Indian folklore, turns up in Europe as Reynard the Fox – to say nothing of his later transmutation into the cartoon character Wiley Coyote, who is always on the point of, but never quite, catching the persecuted and long-suffering 'Roadrunner'. The Sufi tale of the Blind Ones and the Elephant reappears a few centuries later echoed by Rudyard Kipling and others and there are elements of the Christ story, such as the Last Supper, the Resurrection and the Virgin birth which have been repeated constantly in different lands and cultures all over the world.

WHO WERE THE STORYTELLERS?

Before the advent of the written word, storytellers throughout the world were regarded as very special members of the community performing an important and responsible role – that of communicating accurate information to other people. Storytellers were regarded in much the same way as we would regard our modern day newscasters, carrying up to the minute news and spreading the latest gossip!

Because of their importance in the community, storytellers in some cultures were actually required to take a solemn vow in which, among other things, they promised to repeat their stories faithfully and accurately, and also to show respect for their audiences and their interest and enjoyment. This is a tradition which is still in operation today with some recognized groups of storytellers. Perhaps it should be more widespread!

Storytelling was seen as a vocation requiring many skills such as powerful communication, appropriate use of language, insight, sensitivity and accuracy, and in order to do the job well, the storytellers had to develop their own minds in ways that other people at that time did not. They had to develop their own memory and visualization skills, and using these skills, be able to trigger memorable pictures in the minds of their listeners, for it was in this way that the information would be best understood and remembered.

Originally, storytellers would typically be travellers, troubadours or minstrels, who would move from town to town, passing on important information through word, poetry and song. Each would have his own corpus or collection of tales, which would revolve around similar themes – such as the Creation, self-discovery, love, war, magic and the triumph of good over evil.

Over time, these stories would become embellished by each storyteller

3

in his own unique way; each would add his own knowledge and thoughts to the tale, as well as incorporating the latest news as he went along.

More importantly, it was also the traditional role of the storyteller to deal with what might be regarded as difficult truths, uncomfortable issues and complex concepts that were hard for the majority to grasp. They did this by simplifying the topics and finding ways of making them more accessible and palatable to the general public.

Some tales actually contained quite subversive material; the Grail and Arthurian legends, written in the Middle Ages, expressed thoughts and notions that would today be considered as 'alternative' or even 'propagandist' and were contrary to popular and more traditionally held world views.

STORYTELLING TODAY

Stories have had a powerful effect on us all over the world for thousands of years and they continue to be part of our culture today, in terms of helping us to acquire knowledge and enhancing our learning and development. The storytelling tradition is carried on in the modern world both in a 'formal' and 'informal' style.

Stories appear formally in books, movies, newspapers and on television. We hear them in politicians' speeches and in after-dinner talks. Many current day religious rituals and customs originate from ancient myths, and much of the material for Christmas pantomimes dates back to the days of the Arabian nights.

Stories also exist in an informal sense and have been incorporated as part of our everyday language. We only have to think of how often we use such storybook phrases as – 'crying wolf' or 'beauty and the beast', we talk of opening 'Pandora's box' and refer to a weakness as an 'Achilles heel' – to realize that their influence is still there, even though the origins might have long since been forgotten. And those personal anecdotes and jokes that we hear at the bus stop, over dinner and in the pub are all stories in one format or another.

And stories and legends don't have to be about people and issues from the distant past. In modern times we continue to add quite a few of our own – John F. Kennedy, the Loch Ness monster, the fascination with UFOs, to say nothing of royalty stories – have all been put into the melting pot, and will no doubt be given a good stir over the next thousand years.

In a business setting stories can be a particularly potent form of communication – and here again they are used formally – articles in the company newsletter, anecdotes from the Chairman's speech and scenes from the company video, and informally – the factory floor, the canteen, the office and around the car park. They can all have a dramatic effect on the culture of an organization, either positive or negative, depending on the nature and content of the story and who happens to be telling it, and they can encourage change, growth, learning and personal development.

WHO ARE THE STORYTELLERS TODAY?

Do we have modern day storytellers, and if so, who are they? Well, we might not see them dressed in cap and bells as in centuries ago, but nevertheless anyone who is responsible for passing on information to others, encouraging learning and development and who wants to create a powerful message, could still be termed a storyteller. Let's look at where we might find them:

- **On a personal level** Storytellers can be parents, spouses, relatives, friends, colleagues, teachers
- **In a business context** Storytellers can be leaders, managers, directors, trainers, supervisors, consultants, shop stewards
- **In the wider world** Storytellers can be politicians, journalists, entertainers, religious leaders, royalty

This list is not exhaustive and does not include the growing number of professional storytellers, whose work can be enjoyed in schools, theatres and clubs around the United Kingdom. These people can be just as influential as the storytellers of the past.
(For more information on this service, contact the Society for Storytelling, PO Box 2344, Reading RG6 7FG. Tel. 01734 351381.)

THE PURPOSE OF STORIES

A story in its simplest form is an account of an incident or a number of incidents that might be real or imaginary. Although the hero or heroine might be as far-ranging as a chief executive of a company, an all-powerful goddess, to a set of streetwise pigs, the format of stories is basically the same.
    The necessary elements of a good story are:

- character/s
- a plot
- some sort of conflict
- a resolution

All stories contain an adventure of some kind where the hero or heroine is faced with a problem that they endeavour to overcome. If, in addition to pure entertainment value you, as the listener, can identify in some way with the hero or heroine, or if the problems that they are dealing with are similar to your own, then the story will obviously have more significance for you, and you will become much more focused on 'the plot' and 'what happens next?'

It is in this situation, where the listener relates to the story and can draw a parallel between the action in it and his or her own life, and where he or she derives some learning from the underlying message of it, that the story can be called a metaphor.

Stories have been used over the years to educate, inspire, motivate and warn, and particularly before the days of the written word, to pass important information on from one generation to another. Some stories have contained a religious, political or military message, some have commented on the meaning of life. The tone of stories could be romantic, satirical, manipulative and even subversive.

But why did the story become a favourite form of communication above any other? Well, where information could only be passed on orally, obviously a lot depended on human memory – both those telling and those receiving.

Our ancestors did not have the luxury of saying, 'I'll just make a list of these key points' as they moved towards the flip chart, or 'I'll run off a print-out so that you can see more clearly', turning the computer on. Where you couldn't write it down, you had to remember it! And so, oral cultures traditionally placed very high value on any techniques that would help the memory process – rhyme, rhythm, visualization and, of course, story. Kieran Egan, investigating links between learning, memory and the imagination, tells us:

> Of all the techniques invented or discovered for making the lore of a social group securely memorable, by far the most important was the story.
>
> (Egan, 1989)

You might say that story was invented because of the need our ancestors had for accurate memory. The story was a technical tool, not a fanciful notion, which ensured the survival of certain cultures. You can understand how in some cultures this technique became regarded as sacred.

Our ancestors discovered that the way in which stories helped the memory process was by weaving fact in with fantasy and thus stimulating the imagination. They found that the more you could link the information with something outrageous or fantastic, the more likely you were to remember it.

This explains why, in traditional folk tales, it is perfectly normal to come across pigs building houses, tortoises talking to hares, to say nothing of the more fantastical elements of some of the early myths and legends. All modern memory techniques and creative thinking processes that we might think are revolutionary are, in fact, based on the same ancient ideas and have drawn on these same principles.

So, we can appreciate the importance of storytelling for an ancient and illiterate tribe in the South American rain forests, who had no other reliable method of passing information on from one generation to another but, I hear you argue, why have stories remained so popular in our time? What relevance do stories have in our 'high-tech' and (mostly) literate age, where we have any number of ways of communicating our facts, thoughts or feelings to others, and an even larger number of ways of encouraging learning? What is their modern day purpose?

Their purpose and their power are the same as they have always been, although the style, content and emphasis may have changed. A key purpose of stories has been and continues to be to communicate information, to hand down cultural values, to educate, and to give the listener the benefit of some deeper wisdom that will facilitate learning, growth and development. Their power is in motivating us, stirring up our emotions, stimulating our imagination and making us think and reflect on our own lives.

Many stories can be seen in some way as metaphors of life. At a surface level, they provide us with relaxation, enjoyment and a chance to exercise our imagination and memory skills, but at a deeper level, they can help us to deal with the most difficult and complex aspects of our own lives, by offering us a simpler and more positive parallel, helping us to reflect and learn and giving us more choices in how to deal with our own problems. What is 'The Ugly Duckling' after all but a lesson in self-esteem? What is 'The Tortoise and the Hare' but a lesson in time management and planning?

Another reason why we use and apparently enjoy stories so much is that many have happy endings, which leave us in a more positive mood than when we started. And even though consciously we might think of '... and they all lived happily ever after' as an unattainable and not terribly realistic state in today's society, it is nevertheless a state that many of us would still aspire to – for ourselves and others. Nancy Mellon, in her work on the purpose of stories, says:

> In the wise old art of storytelling a 'happy ending' is holy. It cleanses old sorrow and rewards all trials and tribulations. 'And they lived happily ever after' is the equivalent of a triumphant finale.
>
> (Mellon, 1992)

Compare for a moment what thoughts and feelings come into your mind when you hear the '… happy ever after' ending to a story, with the gloom and despondency that descends on you as you watch or listen to or read the daily news. Some psychologists might argue that we shouldn't bury our heads in the sand by living in a fantasy world, that we have to live in the 'here and now'. Certainly we have to live with and accept the realities of life but isn't it good to get a balance of both? Betty Rosen talks about the links and parallels between story and everyday life.

> (In stories) … the real and the extraordinary are constantly shifting places, merging, or staring each other in the face. I suspect that this process is closer than we realize to our own method of making sense of the world for ourselves. … (there is) some psychological rapport with story, because it follows the narrative pattern of normal human speculation.
>
> (Rosen, 1988)

All stories that have a happy ending excite us – whether it be a traditional folk tale, the story your daughter triumphantly tells on her return from school, or the tale you heard at work of how the sales team beat the highest target ever – and give us enthusiasm, courage and optimism for the future. They give us something to feel proud of, something to identify with and something to hope for.

And stories, of course, undoubtedly help to facilitate the learning process for individuals, groups and organizations and they are just as effective for adults as they are for children. I have sometimes been told by cautious trainer colleagues: 'You can't tell stories like *that* to adult groups' and they say it in such a way as though they were describing a new and rather 'whacky' method of teaching.

My answer is that you *can* and *do* tell stories to adults – in the right circumstances and with the right tools – and that when you do you're not introducing any new revolutionary concept, but you are just carrying on a tradition that has gone on for thousands of years.

The use of stories, whether they take the form of traditional folk tales and myths, or whether they are personal anecdotes and analogies, help the learning process by making the information easier for people to understand and remember and by making the information more believable.

THE PURPOSE OF METAPHOR

Whenever we use phrases such as 'My head is as heavy as lead' , or 'It's a minefield out there' or 'Her life was an open book', we are employing the use of metaphor. The definition of metaphor is to 'transfer meaning' ,

8

the word being derived from the Greek *meta* (trans) and *pherein* (to carry). A metaphor is a comparison, a parallel between two, sometimes seemingly unrelated, terms. These terms have been classified as follows:

- The 'topic'   is the original concept
- The 'vehicle'   is its metaphorical equivalent
- The 'ground'   is what the two have in common
- The 'tension'   is the dissimilarity between the two

For example, in the phrase 'My head is as heavy as lead':

- The 'topic'   is *my head*
- The 'vehicle'   is *lead*
- The 'ground'   is what these two domains have in common, eg *a feeling of heaviness*
- The 'tension'   is the dissimilarity between these two domains, eg *head* is flesh, while *lead* is metal

It is this relationship between reality and the two domains that gives metaphor its power in getting a message across to its receiver.

We all use metaphors quite naturally and very often unconsciously in our daily lives, to describe certain events, situations or feelings. We are all familiar with such expressions as, 'He fell at the first hurdle', 'A sea of opportunity awaits you' and 'Caught in a web of deceit' but maybe we're not always fully aware of the powerful effect that this language, whether it is spoken to others or just to ourselves, can have on our thoughts and behaviour.

For example, whether you think of yourself as 'an ugly duckling' or 'a beautiful swan' is going to have some impact on your appearance and how you feel about it! Do you describe yourself as a 'Jack of all trades' or 'master of none'? Do you think of your life as '… a bowl of cherries' or '… a disaster waiting to happen'? Any of these descriptions will naturally have a profound effect on how you develop your own 'model' or understanding of the world and also how you run your life according to that model.

In a learning context specifically, metaphors can be a powerful and innovative way of describing a situation, experience or problem, that can offer alternative information, help the listener to 're-frame' or see that situation in a different light, and hopefully provide them with additional – and sometimes novel – ways of resolving it.

A metaphor can be anything from a simple phrase as mentioned above to a whole story. For example, in Aesop's tale of 'The Sun and the Wind', p. 108, the parallel is between how the sun and wind show off their rela-

9

tive power, to the way in which we handle conflict. The underlying message is that force and aggression – as demonstrated by the wind in the story – is not always the most powerful or indeed effective way of achieving your desired outcome. So, the metaphor in this case works like this:

- The 'topic'   is the *management of conflict*
- The 'vehicle'   is the *sun and the wind proving their power*
- The 'ground'   is what these two domains have in common, eg *the use of different influencing styles*
- The 'tension'   is the dissimilarity between these two domains, eg *elements v. people*

The person listening to the metaphorical story should be able to identify just enough similarity between his or her situation and that of the metaphor to be able to relate to it, but not so much similarity as to dismiss it as being too obvious or overt.

Metaphorical language can be much more powerful and can have a more dramatic effect on the listener than literal language. Imagine for a moment that you were the recipient of the message, 'My love it is a red, red rose ...' It would probably have a more powerful – and hopefully positive – impact on you than if the same person had told you, 'Well, I'm quite fond of you ...'

George Lakoff and Mark Johnson, experts in the use of metaphor, suggest that if a picture is worth 1000 words, then we can think of a metaphor as being worth 1000 pictures. For while a picture provides us with a static image, a metaphor is dynamic, personal and challenging and can provide us with a basis for thinking about and effecting some change in our lives.

> Metaphor is one of our most important tools for trying to comprehend partially what cannot be comprehended totally: our feelings, aesthetic experiences, moral practices and spiritual awareness.
>
> (Lakoff and Johnson, 1980)

THE PURPOSE OF MYTH

Similar to the way in which the meaning of fairy tales has become misunderstood, in modern days the term 'myth' is very often taken to be synonymous with the word 'lie'. But originally it was meant to simply describe a narrative tale, involving a heroic role model – real or imaginary – and was very often set in a supernatural or magical world.

Its purpose originally was to help people make sense of the universe around them, and some of the seemingly unanswerable questions connected with it, which Bruno Bettelheim refers to as:

> …the eternal questions-what is the world really like? How am I to live my life in it? How can I truly be myself?
>
> (Bettelheim, 1991)

In modern times, in the business world, the term 'myth' can apply just as well to those unique sets of stories, rituals and traditions that have been developed and cultivated over a period of time within an organization, and which give it its unique sense of identity.

The purpose of myths today in the business world is to educate people to understand the identity and core values of their organization as well as instructing them in appropriate behaviour – 'The way we do things around here…'

We find in ancient myths there were certain recurrent themes; the tales were intended to answer life questions surrounding such issues as:

- the Creation
- struggle for self-discovery and identity
- battles, warriors and heroes
- love, self-sacrifice, dedication
- wisdom and maturity

Campbell and Moyers (1988), the former an expert on the history of myths, say that 'myths offer life models but the models have to be appropriate to the time in which you are living'. In modern organizational myths, there is a parallel with these ancient themes that can be observed:

The Creation

Many modern day myths revolve around the birth of a company, and include heroic tales of the founders and their early struggles. These are very often 'the good old days' stories; those which remind listeners of the *raison d'être* of the company, why it was created in the first place. When retold, they can be either inspirational or demotivating to the next generation, depending on the current state of morale and health in the organization, and also on who is telling the tale.

Struggle for self-discovery and identity

People love to tell 'survivor' or 'we succeeded in spite of all adversity' stories, where they recount their memories of particular incidents or trau-

11

mas in the company's history, which they not only survived but became better people as a result. An example of this is the 'Setting the World on Fire' story, p. 106, where the group of supervisors discovered a sense of team spirit through the trauma of a factory fire. Struggle for identity can, of course, also relate to the organization itself. I find it quite common to hear people telling 'We just don't know who we are any more' type stories, or 'We've lost our position in the market-place – are we supposed to be a "quality" or a "fast-buck" operation?'

Battles, warriors and heroes

These are usually the myths that are created when the company has gone through a 'bad time' but lived to tell the tale. Many companies who suffered during the recession but survived tell these stories, and of course the 'battles' might be fought internally – department wrangling, industrial action, systems failures, or externally – increased competition, lost orders, etc. The warriors and heroes can be people at any level within the organization who demonstrate courage and fortitude for the good of the company.

Love, self-sacrifice, dedication

People will always revel in myths surrounding the perennial love affairs that go on in organizations, and who did what to whom behind the cycle sheds! But, maybe of more lasting consequence are the myths regarding the selfless love, self-sacrifice and dedication that some employees demonstrate for their company. These might be the people who qualify for long-service awards or best employee of the month, or who are celebrated in the company newsletter or promotional video. But they might just as easily be the 'unsung' heroes, whose selfless deeds very often go unnoticed.

Wisdom and maturity

Myths are told by, and about, an organization's 'elder statesmen', 'tribal leaders' or 'shamans', that is those men and women who have been with the company for many years, maybe even since its creation. They have earned the respect of their peers, and their exploits are retold with almost a reverence, 'There'll never be anyone like him here again.' 'She was a wonderful person; her door was always open, and you could talk to her about anything.' These people are the perpetuators of the company's identity and values, the ones who keep things on the right track, the ones who keep the tribal camp fires burning. They are responsible for instructing the next generation in the company's heritage and sense of tradition, and in what behaviour is consistent with that tradition.

CHAPTER 2

Stories for Learning

IS STORYTELLING STILL VALID?

These days when organizations and individuals are searching for effective, cheaper, longer-lasting and more and more sophisticated ways of helping people to learn – is storytelling still a useful and relevant teaching technique?

As mentioned in Chapter 1, beliefs about the purpose of storytelling have become restricted in recent years, being thought of as belonging purely to the domain of children, but my experience is that stories are still valid and are just as relevant and acceptable to adults as they are to children. They serve as a powerful way of encouraging learning and helping people to make sense of, to understand and experience information and to remember that information more easily.

Peg Neuhauser, in her work with corporations in the United States, found that the learning derived from a well-told story, whether formal or informal, is more likely to be remembered and for far longer than the learning derived from a list of statistical facts or figures.

> Stories allow a person to feel and see the information as well as factually understand it. ... because you 'hear' the information factually, visually and emotionally, it is more likely to be imprinted on your brain in a way that it sticks with you longer, with very little effort on your part.
>
> (Neuhauser, 1993)

And, also, the learning points from a story are very likely to have a 'ripple' effect on others, as the audience is far more likely to repeat the essence of a story to their peers and colleagues than they are the content of a factual report – unless they create their own story out of it!

STORIES AND THE LEARNING PROCESS

Scientist Roger Sperry (1964), identified that we had two sides to the main part of our brain (the cortex) and that each side appeared to be responsible for certain physical and intellectual activities. The right side of the brain, as well as controlling the left-hand side of the body, is responsible for daydreaming, creativity and imagination and our experience of art, colour, music and rhythm. The left side of the brain controls the right-hand side of the body and in addition, such intellectual functions as words, logic, linear thinking and numbers.

But these two halves do not work independently of each other; linking the two halves is a complex mechanism called the corpus callosum that shifts millions of pieces of information backwards and forwards in a very short period of time.

Although individuals have a tendency to be either right- or left-brain dominant, and it is possible through questionnaires such as the Hermann Brain Dominance Instrument to identify which ours is, to label ourselves as 'right brain' or 'left brain' is limiting ourselves, as each of us is actually capable of using both. Perhaps a more useful strategy – particularly in terms of assisting learning – is to identify ways in which the two can be developed and utilized equally. The brain is like any other muscle – if you don't use it, you lose it!

Storytelling requires – for both the storyteller and the listener – the activity of both hemispheres of the brain; the left is involved in processing the words and sequence of the plot and the right in terms of the use of imagination, visualization and creativity.

Roberta and Gerald Evans (1989) investigated ways in which stories, metaphors and analogies might be effective in terms of the following cognitive mechanisms in learning:

- concretizing
- assimilation
- structurizing

CONCRETIZING

Hearing a story helps us to make sense of what might seem an abstract or complex subject through links with tangible or concrete examples. For example, to illustrate the concepts of goal setting, problem solving or benchmarking, you might tell a very simple story like 'The Tube of Toothpaste', p. 74, where individuals find it easy to relate to a very 'real' and concrete situation which is relevant to their own experience.

ASSIMILATION

Learning is a continual process of integrating new information with old information that already exists in our memory. The use of a story, particularly if it is a traditional folk tale, or a story that everyone can relate to, flags up old information in the person's mind that might be seen in new ways. Stories can be particularly useful when introducing a new topic to a group of learners, and they have no similar knowledge to draw on. The story can offer a useful reference point to build on.

For example, the scene from *Alice in Wonderland*, where Alice meets the Cheshire cat, p. 104, is one that is probably universally recognized; most of us have encountered that episode in some form or other during our childhood and, at that time, taken its message at face value. However, when it is reintroduced to us as adults, within the framework of 'goal setting' or 'problem solving', it immediately takes on a more important aspect of a relevant and practical model for current day issues. When I ask group members, 'What does this scene have to do with the way we plan and set goals?' they can all tell me! They are drawing on old, maybe childhood memories as a reference point and then assimilating new information.

STRUCTURIZING

People who are taught with stories can apply the concepts they have been taught to other situations not directly related to the one in which they were taught. In other words, they are building new structures of knowledge and can generalize to other areas beyond the time and place of instruction.

For example, in the story of 'The Enormous Turnip', p. 90, the group who analysed it (see Chapter 3) were able to extrapolate a number of key learning points applying directly to the main topic of teambuilding, and which also applied to more general areas of management, such as influencing and communication.

Roberta and Gerald Evans (1989) carried out a number of experiments with two groups of undergraduate students. Both groups were given a lecture 45 minutes long, but in one group stories, metaphors and analogies were used and in the other they weren't. Both groups were given pre- and post-test questions.

Their results showed that first of all, those taught with stories demonstrated fewer conceptual and technical errors than those taught without. And secondly, that those taught with stories showed that they were more capable of structurizing the information, that is applying the concepts of what they had learnt to more far-reaching and novel situations, than those taught without.

Another researcher, P. R. J. Simons (1984), investigated the power of story and concrete analogies with regard to learning when teaching quite complex subjects such as electricity. He tested 61 students, made up of elementary and secondary school pupils and college students, and followed the teaching with a 40-item, multiple choice test, with factual knowledge questions.

He found that teaching using stories and concrete analogies led to improved performance in all students. The results of the tests showed that those who had learnt with stories had a more tangible grasp of the topic and a better idea of the relationship between concepts than did students learning without them.

METAPHORS AND LEARNING

Although I tend to use the term 'story' to encompass metaphors and analogies, I think it is worth looking specifically at how metaphorical language can be used in the context of learning. It is a part of human speech that is becoming more widely accepted and recognized as a way of helping people to acquire new knowledge, and helping them to transfer learning from what is well known to what is less well known in a vivid and memorable way.

Andrew Ortony (1993), investigating the uses of metaphor, maintains that there are three main reasons for using metaphor in our everyday lives and particularly in a learning context, namely:

- to achieve *compactness* in how we communicate
- to include *vividness* in our language
- to help us express *the inexpressible*

Compactness

We use metaphor in our language because it is quick, concise and effective, and can be used to provide universal understanding. For example, if a woman said to you, 'I'm so frightened, I'm a jelly inside', the statement itself would not stand up to scientific analysis. The woman does not expect to be taken literally, and would be horrified if people set upon her armed with bowls and spoons! But the statement is one which we could all understand, and most of us could relate to. 'I'm a jelly inside' is actually a shorthand version of 'I'm feeling anxious, tense, nervous, my body is shaking with fear, I feel that someone could easily knock me over.'

Vividness

Metaphors provide us with vivid symbols and images, which very often spark off our emotions, and make the content which they describe more easily understood. In addition the information becomes more credible and more easily remembered. For example, 'He was a roaring tiger when he met his opponent' immediately conjures up a vivid mental image of the scene, certainly more so than if we had been told 'He looked pretty confident.'

In addition to this, the vividness of a metaphor helps to develop our thinking and stimulates our imagination. Vivid metaphors help us to describe and understand different types of leader – whether they are 'shark', 'dolphin', 'pussy cat' or 'Attila the Hun'. They can help us to categorize different types of team member – 'salt of the earth' or 'snake in the grass'. And they can also give us a clear picture of a particular type of organization – 'riding in the fast lane', 'Cinderella outfit', or 'set of cowboys.'

Inexpressibility

Metaphors can help us to add clarity to issues which are difficult to describe and express succinctly in prosaic language. We talk in terms of 'speaking metaphorically' when we experience difficulty in getting a point across. 'This job is either feast or famine' or 'My job is a series of plates on sticks – trying to keep them all balanced at the same time' might be useful metaphors for describing the transient and ephemeral nature of one person's job.

In terms of the learning process, metaphors – whether simply a short phrase, or part of a whole story – are an innovative way of describing a potentially difficult situation and offering new ways of resolving it by changing the person's view of the relationship between the problem and the metaphor.

They can be useful when encouraging individuals to analyse and maybe change their views about themselves and their levels of self-esteem. I have a set of cards that I use for this, which have written on statements such as:

If you were a *cartoon character*, what would you be?
If you were a *Christmas present*, what would you be?
If you were a *smell*, what would you be?
If you were a *drink*, what would you be?

The answers I get from groups are both amusing and enlightening! Let me share with you the comments from a group who were working on assertiveness and personal development:

Cartoon character	'I'm all the characters in Looney Tunes, because I'm flexible, I'm good fun, and I'm not the grim-faced person they paint me out to be'
Christmas present	'I'm a teddy bear, because I'm soft and cuddly and I like to get lots of affection'
Smell	'I'm the smell of roast beef, because that's what makes my husband come running!'
Drink	'I'm water, because it's important, it supports life and it's pure'

You can see from the above that when asked 'Why?' the answers are illuminating and in some cases, quite profound – both in terms of what knowledge they offer the individual themselves and also in terms of what knowledge or insight might be offered for their colleagues.

A word of warning here, although these types of games are good fun, and I have found that all the groups I have used them with enjoy them and get a lot out of them, I think it unwise to underestimate the profundity of what you are doing. People are baring their souls here – even though it's done in a jocular way – and you may find that some are more willing than others to do that. I usually start the ball rolling by offering the group *my* contribution, which is partly to give them the idea of the nature of the game, and partly to demonstrate that I am equally prepared to share a personal view.

Metaphor-based games like this can also be used in a similar way to help individuals rethink their relationship with each other, with other departments or indeed with their organization.

When posed with the question, 'If your boss were the course of a meal, what would he/she be?', the young manager thought for a long time, and then said very definitely and seriously, 'Oh, he would have to be the pudding.' 'How do you work that out?' one of his colleagues queried. 'Oh you know, ' he continued, 'sometimes you feel like him and sometimes you don't!'

His answer produced much laughter and applause from his peers who, knowing the individual concerned, could immediately relate to his observation. And for those of you who might be thinking, 'That sounds a little condemnatory', I should point out that this was an organization with very positive views on such issues as 360° appraisal and open communication, and that the 'boss' in question was also present in the group and laughed along with the rest.

Using metaphors as part of learning can also be particularly useful if you are working with groups of people who don't share the same culture, knowledge or values, and where mutual understanding might be difficult to attain. This could range from a learning group made up from neigh-bouring departments in one organization, where there is no sense of shared values or understanding, to working with a learning group made up of people from different ethnic, religious or gender backgrounds.

Lakoff and Johnson say that metaphors have a valuable role to play in these situations, in that they encourage mutual understanding through the negotiation of meaning and the valuing of diversity.

> Metaphorical imagination is a crucial skill in creating rapport and in com-municating the nature of unshared experience. This skill consists, in large measure, of the ability to bend your world view and adjust the way you cat-egorise your experience.
>
> (Lakoff and Johnson, 1980)

A colleague of mine was involved in a 'think-tank' in her organization, made up of the senior managers from all the varying departments, the purpose being to debate the organization's current and future direction. After several, not particularly successful, attempts to gain commitment through a literal description of her vision of the future, my friend resorted to metaphor:

> Look, imagine we're a stream: it starts way up in the hills somewhere as a tiny trickle, then as it rushes down the hill, it gathers momentum and also collects other streams on its way. So it becomes bigger. And now it's become so big, that there is white water and rapids, and in those rapids, some people get lost or drown or get bashed against the rocks. But they also pro-vide great energy as the river continues to flow out to the sea ...

Because the imagery was vivid and powerful, and the 'vehicle' that she chose, ie the water, was universally recognized, her colleagues could instantly relate to her ideas. I'm curious to know whether anybody talked about 'taking them on board!'

MYTHS AND LEARNING

Just as we have become accustomed to the term 'the learning organiza-tion' people are now beginning to talk about the concept of 'the story-telling organization' (Boje, 1991) and to recognize the importance of organizational myths in terms of shaping culture and in providing a powerful tool for learning. Not all stories that are told within organizations necessarily become myths: these are particular stories that develop over a period of time, which feature heroic characters and deeds, and that are handed down from one generation to another to become part of the tradition and history of the organization.

People tell modern day myths in organizations just as they did in ancient times and for just the same reasons, namely to answer 'difficult' questions, whether it be about the meaning of life or the existence of an organization. These days myths help us to:

- determine the identity and values of the organization
- shape its vision and goals for the future
- learn and adopt the behaviour that is consistent with the organization's identity
- learn and abide by its rules and taboos
- bring about necessary change in people and culture

People within every organization tell their own myths, unique to them, which involve the identification of their own corporate heroic or legendary figures who serve as role models for others working their way up the ladder. These legendary characters are just as likely to be current members of the organization – a 'legend in their own time' – as they are people who have long since retired, maybe even founded the company . They might be chief executive officers (CEOs) or managing directors, but, particularly with the introduction of more flattened hierarchies, could just as easily be the shop steward, supervisor, administration assistant or cleaner. Mythology does not take account of status!

But whoever they are, what all these modern day heroes have in common is that in some way they have demonstrated an aspect of the organization's identity, values or beliefs; they have given a tangible example that others can learn from and emulate.

One modern myth I particularly like is that of a chief executive of a national retailing company in Britain. He had a rule for all his management team that when visiting a store, they should park in an area of the car park that was furthest away from the store. There were two reasons for this rule:

1. The parking spaces nearest to the store were for the use of customers as they were the most important people to the company.
2. Parking at the bottom of the car park would give the manager concerned a 'customer's eye view' of the car park and the approach to the store.

The story goes that on one particular day the chief executive was visiting a store, and just as he arrived, the heavens opened up and there was a downpour of torrential rain. Rather than compromise his own standards, the chief executive parked his car in his usual spot at the bottom of the car park, and walked (or probably ran) to the store – a distance of a good 200 yards. By the time he got there he was soaked to the skin and the store management, trying not to laugh, offered him some dry clothes.

Now, I'm sure that as this myth is told and retold by countless generations of employees in this company, it will become more and more embroidered and no doubt produce a few giggles at the chief executive's expense. But the moral of the tale, which is what makes it in my view so powerful, is that in spite of the weather conditions and in spite of his obvious status and power, this man did not sacrifice the principles he had set for himself and his management team, but continued to behave in a way that was consistent with them. And this is the learning that others will derive from this story and which will become part of the company's culture.

Compare the above story with this one of another chief executive of a large manufacturing company based in the north of England, who also *said* that customers were the most important people to his business. The first impression that any customer receives when visiting their head office is being confronted by walls, barriers and broken glass all around the site, but there is no sign to indicate the name of the company, which means that the customer has to get out of their car and walk up to the security box to verify if they are in the right place.

The next task for the intrepid customer is to find the visitors' parking space – yes, you've guessed! It is in the roughest, muddiest part of the car park, a good 200 yards from the main reception building. And the final insult for the customer – if they've survived the long walk through the mud and gravel – comes when they approach the main building. It is almost impossible to walk up the flight of steps to the front entrance – why? Because the chief executive's car is parked right on the very edge of the steps which means that any remaining customers, who have still retained the will to live, have to squeeze down between the side of the car and the bordering hedge to gain access to the front door.

Now, who could blame the employees of the second company for their 'devil may care' attitude to customers? For, in spite of the grandiose mission statements and quality policies, they know what their chief executive *really* thinks – he tells them that every morning as they come in for work. They learn far more from that demonstration from him than they ever did from any customer care course!

These are the kinds of myth that pervade every organization and teach the next generation of employees what sort of behaviour is acceptable and what is unacceptable. Myths can be positive or negative, and of course they might be true or untrue, but one thing is certain: if the behaviour that is demonstrated within the organization does not match the story that is being told, then the story, and probably the storyteller, will have no credibility with the audience and the only lesson to be learnt will be not to trust the stories that you hear! It is the fusing together of the myth and the observed behaviour that is what teaches people the principle.

Probably the most important factor with regard to the creation and telling of organizational myths is that *you cannot stop it happening!* People in organizations are always going to tell these types of story to each other that have particularly inspired or moved them – either in a positive or negative way. This process is one of the most powerful and underestimated forms of human communication, and the challenge to people in organizations is to be aware that it is happening and to utilize the process in the most productive way.

So, what can you, as a trainer or manager do to utilize the myths in your organization in order to encourage the learning process? Where and when might they best be employed?

- **Where and when are the myths already being told?** Be prepared to listen to what types of myth are being told and perpetuated in your company, and find out where and when they are being passed on to others. Are the myths positive or negative? What do they teach about the company? Who are the heroes? Who is the enemy?
- **On induction courses** This is a good opportunity to demonstrate to new employees what the organization's values and corresponding behaviours are. It's a more effective way to learn this from a respected storyteller, who tells 'creation' and 'battles, warriors and heroes' type stories rather than through reading faceless hand-outs or through clinical promotional videos. In one manufacturing company I worked in, we would invite a 'resident' manager to every induction programme purely to come and retell the company myths and legends.
- **Company newsletters** Although many myths tend to be told rather than written, this is still a powerful medium to include any 'struggle for self-discovery and identity' or 'love, self-sacrifice and dedication' type stories, and the more vivid and colourful the better!
- **Customer/client meetings** Retelling old 'creation' or 'wisdom and maturity' tales reinforces the stability of the company.
- **Social events** When people are relaxed, and able to step out of their day-to-day routine, they are usually more vocal than in a formal meeting; indeed this is where some of your most powerful myths may be born!
- **Team briefing sessions** This is a good opportunity to applaud

people's success using 'struggle for self-discovery and identity' tales, 'battles, warriors and heroes' tales or 'love, self-sacrifice and dedication' tales. These stories could be relating to people in your own department, where you might encourage them to 'tell their own heroic story' or telling the story of someone in another department.

- **Other training events** Any in-house training can be a golden opportunity to re-establish the core values and mores of the company, through utilizing the whole range of different types of myth, and encouraging participants to tell their own.

In more general terms, the teaching from modern myths is available to all of us in such classic management books as *How to Win Friends and Influence People* (Carnegie, 1936), *In Search of Excellence* (Peters and Waterman, 1982) and more recently, *Maverick!* (Semler, 1993), *First Person* (Teal, 1996) and a growing fleet of books by Canfield and Hansen (1993) under the generic term *Chicken Soup for the Soul*.

In these books, we read tales of courage and tenacity featuring heroic men and women who were successful in spite of great adversity. We learn of heroic leaders whose style was inspirational, and we hear of heroic achievements in such areas as customer care, quality and communication that are just as thrilling, memorable and educational in their way as any we are likely to find from Greece or Rome.

Thomas Teal, in his introduction to the book *First Person*, actually likens CEOs of some companies to the heroes of the Romantic age:

> ... their isolation, their single-mindedness, the fact that they are perpetually swimming against the current, against the wishes of one or more of their supporters, against convention, against heavy odds.
>
> (Teal, 1996)

THE HIDDEN MESSAGE OF STORIES

One burning question in relation to the use of stories in learning, particularly those that are metaphorical in nature, is 'To tell or not to tell?' Do you as the trainer or manager divulge the message that is implicit within the story you have just told? Do you say nothing and leave people to ponder on their own thoughts and interpretations? Do you assume that your listeners have 'heard' the same message as you? Or do you hold a discussion to debate what the message *might* be?

There is no easy answer to this question, and many authors have written outlining their different points of view on the subject. Thomas Sticht (1993) argues that mass-produced stories can be dangerous in a learning environment, because there might be so many individual interpretations as to jeopardize the quality of the learning; he maintains that you as the storyteller are trying to bring about clarity, not create a state of excessive puzzlement in your learners.

Hugh Petrie and Rebecca Oshlag (1993) on the other hand argue that it is through the very puzzlement of metaphor that clarity emerges. They see the effect of stories in learning as a four-step process:

1. The 'anomaly' step	where the student sees the situation as a problem and knows that he/she needs to do something to ease the situation
2. Providing the metaphor	the student hears a story either from a story-teller or through reading a textbook
3. Acting out the metaphor	the student behaves in the new way that the story would suggest, and decides if the original anomaly has been removed
4. Correcting the activity	in the light of the results the student gets from his/her new behaviour, further adjustments may have to be made to remove the original anomaly completely

My own feeling on the 'to tell or not to tell' debate is that first of all you, as the storyteller, have to be clear as to what purpose you want the story to serve, and how important you think it is in terms of that purpose, that your audience receives the same message that you intended.

- If you are using the story as a relaxing end to the day, then it is probably advisable to leave people in their relaxed state, and allow them to reflect and ponder on the meaning. Some examples of stories that fit into this category would be:

  'The Prophet' p. 122
  'Giant Steps' p. 120
  'Autobiography in Five Short Chapters' p. 110
  'Atlas' Tale' p. 170
  'The Ball of Wool' p. 114

- If the story is a very short 'throw-away' anecdote or metaphor, humorous in nature and where the message is fairly simplistic, then it is advisable to leave the message unspoken. You would probably spoil the element of surprise and humour by labouring the point, and also it is easy to antagonize an audience by demonstrating that you don't really

25

trust their capabilities of comprehension. You can tell by your audience's reaction – verbal or non-verbal – as to whether they've 'got it'. Some examples of stories that fit into this category would be:

'What the Sleeping Beauty would have given her Right Arm for' p. 76
'The Tube of Toothpaste' p. 74
'Sophie learns a lesson' p. 82
'And I'm not Joking!' p. 72
'Percy the Pot' p. 80
'All Those Buns!' p. 155

- If the story's purpose is to offer a tangible example of a theory you are discussing, then it is advisable to ask your audience in a fairly light-hearted style: 'So, what on earth does this story have to do with ... goal setting/motivation?' or 'What relevance do you think that story has to what we've been discussing?' (Don't ask the favourite question: 'Do you understand?' It tells you nothing in terms of the group's comprehension, and can be seen as insulting into the bargain!) Allow the group to offer you their understanding of the message, and draw the links between that and their own experience. Some examples of stories that fit into this category would be:

'Alice Meets the Cheshire Cat' p. 104
'Waste Paper' p. 98
'Mother and the Knife Grinder' p. 94
'Leave Well Alone' p. 128
'Lessons from the Geese' p. 136

- If your story is helping to clarify an already complex or broad topic, then it is probably advisable to explain the link that *you* see between the story and the topic you are discussing, to ensure consistency in the learning. Some examples of stories that fit into this category would be:

'The Cookery Book Game' p. 84
'There is no Such Thing as a "Difficult Delegate"' p. 102
'The Meaning of my Communication' p. 78
'Did I Tell you the One About...?' p. 112

- If you are using the story as the basis for a case study or group discussion, then the question for the groups to debate is 'What do you understand as being this story's message, and how is it relevant to ... teambuilding/quality management?' When the groups feed back their understanding is when you can open up the discussion, compare their understanding with your own, and iron out any anomalies. Some examples of stories that fit into this category would be:

It is worth remembering that any person who is listening to a story will always make their own interpretations and draw out their own personal message – so does the storyteller – and so does the writer! This is why in Part Two of this book, I have outlined in the 'Moral' and 'Reflection' parts which follow every story, what *I* believe to be the message or messages of the story and where it might best be used in a learning context. You as the storyteller then make the decision as to:

(a) what *you* think the message is
(b) where you want to use the story and for what purpose
(c) whether or not you tell your group the message

The choice is yours!

STORY AND MEMORY

Although there has been much discussion about memory over the years we can define it simply as the retention and retrieving of prior learning. Psychologists have identified that our memories seem to work best in these ways:

- where we can see things as part of a recognized order or pattern
- where our imaginations and emotions are aroused
- where we can make natural associations between one idea and another
- where the information appeals strongly to our senses – seeing, hearing, smelling, tasting and feeling

So, what part can storytelling play in encouraging the development of our memory?

Where we can see things as part of a recognized order or pattern

Our brains quite naturally seek out pattern, completion and wholeness. Psychologists refer to this phenomenon as a 'gestalt'. This explains why, when someone sneezes, we automatically say 'Bless you', or why we would find it hard to hear the sentence 'A Mars a day ...' without adding as if by rote '... helps you work, rest and play'. It also explains why, for some people, it is difficult to resist the urge to finish off someone else's sentence for them. 'I thought today we might … uuh …' 'Go to the pictures? Read a book? Emigrate?' you add helpfully.

The same is true in storytelling terms. Because of this natural tendency to look for pattern and completion, we find it easy to remember what are known as 'cumulative' stories, that is where there is repetition and build up of certain words or phrases. This is why as children we particularly enjoyed and remembered stories like 'The Gingerbread Man' and 'Red Riding Hood'. We begin to recognize and anticipate the repetition of the same phrases (Who *doesn't* remember – 'Oh, Grandmama, what big *eyes* you have!') and a pattern begins to form in the mind that makes recall easier. ('The Enormous Turnip' is a good example of a cumulative tale.)

The same process is equally true in adult tales; the more you can include in any stories or anecdotes the repetition of words, phrases, or maybe even a character (real or imaginary) the more the content will be committed to memory, and the easier will be the recall. Be aware, however, as to what it is you are repeating – is it a positive message? And be careful not to overdo this technique: one trainer I knew who had recently moved jobs, referred to his 'old' company so often during one training seminar that the delegates started counting and, of course, while their brains were focused on that, they weren't focused on anything else!

Equally, the practice of starting one story and finishing it later (see Chapter 3) creates a 'gestalt' in your audience, which arouses the level of curiosity and intrigue as to how to story ends.

Where our imaginations and emotions are aroused

Scientists have now proved that, as well as having two halves to our brains, we also have three levels from the top to the brain stem. The upper brain, the 'cortex', previously mentioned, controls our intellectual processes such as thinking, talking and so on. The lower brain, known as the 'reptilian', controls much of our instinctive behaviour, such as breathing; and the central part, the 'limbic system', is responsible for our emotions.

Scientists have also shown that the limbic system is situated near to that part of the brain responsible for memory storage, which explains how we tend to remember information more easily if our emotions are involved.

So, when using story as a learning tool, the more the content activates the imagination, through the inclusion of novel situations, fantastic creatures or mythical beings, and stirs the emotions – humour, pathos, empathy – the more likely the message is to be remembered.

Another theory about being told a story is that the process itself can bring about in us a form of regression to childhood days, and subsequently recreates in us that emotional state of curiosity which is ever present in children, but which as adults we tend to lose. Once in this childlike state, we tend to be more receptive and interested in the information we are given and thus commit more to memory.

Where we can make natural associations between one idea and another

We know that the brain is made up of billions of neurons or nerve cells, each with a central point and branches called 'dendrites', radiating off the centre like a tree. Each of these neurons stores information and transmits it to other neurons adjacent to it by means of an electrical chemical charge.

So, every time you say, 'I've had a flash of inspiration!' or 'The idea came to me like a bolt from the blue!', you're quite right. What we refer to glibly as 'thinking' is actually an incredibly complicated network of these electrical charges, shooting from one neuron to another countless numbers of times every day.

This is why memories are made easier to recall if we can associate them with something else. How many of us, if asked how many days there are in June, could honestly give the answer without referring, albeit silently, to the jingle 'Thirty days hath September ...'

Some 'association games' like these are universal, others we develop to suit ourselves. For example, many people that I meet on training courses have devised their own, sometimes ingenious, methods for remembering names.

However, this was not so for the poor woman who told me her story of what she thought was a very clever way of remembering the name 'Robinson'. 'It was easy,' she said, 'I told myself to remember the character Robinson Crusoe, and that would have worked well ... until I called him "Mr Crusoe" by mistake.' Our memory recall is not always infallible!

Brainstorming exercises work in this way; hearing an idea from one person triggers an associated thought in another. And anyone who is familiar with Tony Buzan's (1993) invention of 'Mind Maps' will recognize the same process. Tony encourages the inclusion of colour, visual images, symbols and codes to stimulate this associative function of the brain.

Listening to stories can also help our brains in that naturally occurring function of making associations. They encourage us to associate one word with another word, or with a picture, sound or feeling. In the same way that we use visual images in our mind maps, we cannot stop ourselves, when listening to a story, from creating visual images only this time we do it inside our mind not outside it.

Where the information appeals strongly to our preferred sense

Students of neuro-linguistic programming (NLP) will be familiar with the notion that people process thought, communicate, learn and remember through use of the five senses:

- visual
- auditory
- kinesthetic
- olfactory
- gustatory

and that each of us tends to have one preferred sense, or 'representational system', the most common being visual, auditory or kinesthetic. What this means in terms of learning and memory is that different individuals will respond to different types of stimuli, depending on what their representational system is.

Visual learners are happiest learning when they can see things written down, are watching videos or are shown diagrams or models on a flip chart, overhead projector or in text form. Their language is indicative of what is going on in their brain: 'I get the picture', 'I don't see the point of this', etc.

Auditory learners are happiest learning through lectures, group discussions, audio-cassettes and, of course, storytelling! The sort of language they use is: 'I hear what you say' or 'I like the sound of that'.

Kinesthetic learners are happiest learning when experiencing feelings, sensations or physical activity, so 'role play', training 'games' and outward bound courses are ideal for them. They use language like 'I feel good about this', 'I'm really excited about the future.'

Eric Jensen, author of the book, *Superteaching*, (1988), has found that in any learning group, you can expect 40 per cent of your learners to be predominantly visual, 40 per cent to be auditory and 20 per cent kinesthetic. When we trigger an individual's preferred sense and relate to it, we make their processing of information and subsequent recall of that information easier.

Obviously it is difficult to cater for each person as an individual, so this is where the use of storytelling can help, as it can appeal to all three representational systems.

The 'visual learner' will remember most of your story if they can make internal pictures as they listen, or they may like to see the text of your story, if you have one. It was interesting that when I used a story as a case study with a large medical company in the north of England (see Chapter 3), although the two groups involved were both offered a copy of the script, only one group asked to see it, and spent some time highlighting certain passages. The other group relied on their memories of my telling the tale.

The 'auditory learner' will remember most by concentrating on the voice of the storyteller, 'hearing' any sounds that figure in your story, together with any other internal sounds that may be going through their mind. Auditory learners very often tell me how much they enjoyed listening to my voice at the end of a training session, adding the comment rather warily, 'You don't hypnotize people do you?' The auditory learner, of course, also responds well to taped stories, discussion and reading to themselves.

The 'kinesthetic learner' will remember most by making links and associations between the content of the story and their own emotions and feelings. It is not uncommon, from my experience, to see the kinesthetic members of the group (both male and female) become quite emotional if they are listening to a story such as 'Giant Steps', p. 120 or 'The Prince and the Magician' p. 118 or some of the *Parables*, and they very often come up to me afterwards, shake me fondly by the hand and say wistfully, 'I really enjoyed the story – it made me feel so relaxed!'

In some cases, a good story might encapsulate all of the different memory triggers mentioned above. I remember during an interactive presentation skills course, one group decided to conduct their own experiment. They split the audience into two; one half was asked to memorize a list of some 20 everyday objects purely by hearing them read out in a random fashion, while the other half was shown the objects and at the same time listened to a story into which all the objects were woven as part of the story.

The story that the group had written was imaginative and creative in content, vivid in its use of imagery and above all humorous. There were many delightful puns included such as when the storyteller said, while holding up a teaspoon, '… her feelings stirred …'

At the end of the experiment, the group who had been told the story could remember many more of the items than those who had just heard a random list. And another interesting addendum to the story was that when the two groups compared notes, some of the 'listening' group admitted that they had been thinking up stories or categories in their own minds.

STORY AND UNCONSCIOUS LEARNING

We now know that in order for different parts of the brain to send their electronic messages backwards and forwards to other parts, they use different 'frequencies' or brainwaves – a bit like the way we tune in our television sets to different channels! The four different levels of brain activity are:

- Beta   The conscious, wide-awake mind
          Operates at 14–21 cycles per second
- Alpha   Relaxed awareness
          Operates at 7–14 cycles per second
- Theta   On the edge of sleep
          Operates at 4–7 cycles per second
- Delta   Deep sleep
          Operates at 0.5–4 cycles per second

You might think that the faster our minds were working, ie the Beta level, the faster our minds would take in information, learn and remember but we know now that this is not the case. Scientists have proved that much of what we learn and remember is not necessarily the same as what we are being 'taught'.

We only have to think of how many advertising slogans and jingles we can repeat by heart, to realize how much information we apparently take in – almost accidentally – while our attention is focused on something else.

Much of our learning is, in fact, taken in at an unconscious level, and paradoxically, it is the slower brainwaves, particularly the alpha and theta levels, that trigger the unconscious mind and produce feelings of well-being and relaxed awareness. It is in this particular state that we allow our minds to 'wander' and to daydream and we experience feelings of heightened concentration. We are able to use our creative imagination more freely and, of course, we are most receptive to learning.

This was the principle used by Bulgarian psychologist Dr Georgi Lozanov (1979), who, in the 1950s, created 'suggestopedia', or, as it has become better known, 'accelerated learning systems'. Lozanov discovered that students learnt and memorized information most effectively if their brainwaves were reduced to approximately 7–14 cycles per second, ie the alpha level, and he found that one particularly effective way of inducing this state was by playing certain types of music, that is music whose rhythm helped to slow down the heart beat to 50–70 beats per minute. Lozanov found that the baroque school – featuring composers such as Bach, Handel and Vivaldi – produced the best effects.

We can access the deeper levels of alpha and theta by using other techniques such as relaxation, deep breathing, meditation and, of course, storytelling. Listening to a story is a very natural method of helping to reduce our brain's activity; as well as scientific evidence, ask any parent who is trying to get their child to go to sleep about the soporific qualities of storytelling!

In a business context, listening to a story – whether in a formal or informal setting – is seen by most people as a non-threatening activity; it does not require any active participation, and does not involve any risk, unlike the dreaded role play or more traditional 'ice-breaker' exercises! Listening to a story simply induces feelings of relaxed awareness and makes people more receptive to learning.

The power of storytelling lies in the fact that in listening to the content, our conscious mind is occupied, leaving our unconscious mind open to directly receive the underlying message or moral. As storytellers, we must be aware of this power, and ensure that the stories we tell have a positive effect on our listeners.

CHAPTER 3

The Right Time and Place

WHOSE STORY IS IT ANYWAY?

Everyone likes to think they are a good raconteur but unfortunately not everybody is! We've all suffered at the hands of the party bore, the person who holds us hostage in the kitchen and recites long passages from comedy shows such as *Monty Python*, *Blackadder* or *Cheers*, that were incredibly funny – the first time round. And we've all met the person who tells us tale after tale of unspeakable tedium, each one prefixed with the line '… and this one is *really* funny …' which you can take to be a sure fire guarantee that it won't be.

And equally frustrating is the friend, who after you have just launched into your personal epic tale of love, woe, deceit and despair, replies with, 'Don't talk to me about your problems. Wait till I tell you *my* story …'

In a business context, you have to remember that whether it is a training seminar, management conference or team meeting, if you are the leader of the team, you too have a captive audience. But this is no excuse for treating them as 'kitchen hostages'. I'm sure there are many tales and anecdotes that you would love to tell but are they relevant? Are they as enjoyable for your audience as they are for you? What purpose do they serve? And who are they helping most – you or the listener?

I remember one storyteller who admitted (after the event) that the hour long story he recounted was mainly for personal therapeutic purposes rather than for the edification and delight of his audience. If he had had any sensitivity at all he would have observed certain members of the team slipping slowly and silently down in their chairs heading straight towards oblivion.

Betty Rosen (1988), a professional storyteller, says that it's not enough to find a story which is personally appealing, and which *you* want to tell; it also has to be right for your audience and this is particularly true in a business context and with adult learners. The key to picking the 'right time and place' for telling a story is being able to put yourself into not just the shoes, but also the mind of the recipient and considering their needs before your own.

In the communications model known as neuro-linguistic programming – devised by Richard Bandler and John Grinder in America in the 1970s – they call this process going into 'second position' and this means imagining yourself taking on the physiology of the other person, and seeing, hearing and feeling the world as if you were in their shoes.

If you are considering telling a story or analogy or using a metaphor as part of a training session, or business conference, try out this exercise beforehand. Make sure, however, that you do it before your audience arrives!

First position

- Sit in the chair that you will be occupying, or stand where you are going to stand to tell your story.
- Imagine in your mind that you are telling the story, and observe the imaginary audience.
- Then ask yourself – what do I see, hear and feel?
- In the light of the information you get, could you change your behaviour to make the experience more effective?

Second position

- Now go and sit in at least one of the seats that your audience will be occupying. If you know any of them, so much the better, but if you don't, just act as if you did.
- Really imagine that you are *them*, watching and listening to *you* telling the story.
- Then ask yourself – now what do I see, hear and feel?
- In the light of the information you get, could the person telling the story change their behaviour to make the experience more effective for you?

Like any other skill, storytelling requires preparation in order to look effortless, and practise to ensure that it is used in exactly the right time and place, and for the right reasons. I think back – with crimson face – to the time when I told my group what I thought to be a funny anecdote about the perils of recruiting family members in the same organization. It *was* funny until I discovered that the young, smug looking woman sitting at the back of the room was in fact the managing director's daughter!

Storytelling can be a wonderful management tool but like any other it can be overused or exploited. You must be aware of any cues that your audience is giving you: for example, if your enthusiastic introduction of '… and that reminds me of *another story*!' is not greeted with equal enthusiasm from your audience, but with universal groans – then you know that you've overdone it!

Beware also of thinking that you have the monopoly on storytelling; you will probably find that if you adopt a more anecdotal style, your group will follow your lead, and will want to contribute their own experiences. Do encourage them to do this: not only is it increasing their level of involvement and enjoyment, but obviously there is twice the learning potential for you as well as for the group.

All storytelling is made up of three variable elements:

- the story
- the storyteller
- the audience

Where there is harmony and balance between these three variables, storytelling can be a wonderful and educational way of gaining rapport with a learning group. To help you achieve this harmony and decide on the best time and place, you may find it useful to go through this checklist in your mind before you start:

- What purpose do I want this story to serve – inspire, educate, illustrate a point, energize or relax the recipient?
- Does storytelling fit in with this organization's culture?
- What sort of story will be most appropriate – folk talk, personal anecdote, myth?
- What message am I trying to convey – communication, team work, motivation?
- What particular story might help their understanding right now?
- Is there a metaphor that would help them see things a different way?
- Should I read a story or just retell it in my own words?

WHEN CAN YOU TELL STORIES?

Whatever sort of educator role you have in business, you should be aware that stories, metaphors and myths are *already* being told in your organization, by all manner of people, and in virtually any situation – formal and informal. And that storytelling is a very powerful, and up until now, largely underestimated management tool.

It sometimes intrigues me as to how much money companies invest today in such areas as external recruitment advertising, while at the same time totally ignoring the largest and most influential advertising campaign that is being waged inside their four walls – the stories that their own employees tell to each other and to friends and colleagues. Of course, this is the way organizations very quickly pick up a good or bad reputation, depending on the 'informal' stories that are being told.

One reason for the power of storytelling in organizations is that, particularly in an informal setting, there are no rules to cover it in the company procedures manual and, of course, you cannot legislate for the content of the stories that people tell! So if, as trainers or managers, we become more aware of the existence of and the power of storytelling, we can find ways to use it and manage it more positively.

In formal settings

Stories can be used to great effect in training seminars, management conferences, team meetings, away days, recruitment or appraisal interviews, induction training, organizational videos and newsletters.

In informal settings

Stories are told informally anywhere where people congregate in organizations, for example in staff cafeterias, car parks, on the factory floor, in offices, in meetings with colleagues, in meetings with customers and suppliers and, of course, during social events.

Let's focus on the formal settings for storytelling when you, as a trainer, are consciously incorporating stories, metaphors, myths or anecdotes as a means of assisting learning or effecting change with a group or an individual and identify how and in what situations they might best be used.

Before the event

If you are holding a training seminar, staff conference or team meeting, one idea is to contact each member a couple of weeks before and ask them to read the text of a story before they come to the event. *But* a couple of warnings here. If you decide to try out this method, do make sure that the story is appropriate, that it has some relevance to the event itself and most important, that you remember the story yourself, and utilize or at least refer to it in some way during the course of the day.

My experience shows that groups have no objection to undertaking pre-course work as long as the trainer acknowledges and praises the fact that they have done it, and that delegates can see the purpose to it and how it fits in with the general theme, ideas or learning of the day.

A private health care company I worked with gave all their employees a copy of a book on empowerment, prior to attending a seminar on that subject. It was certainly a very powerful and innovative way of setting the scene for the training seminar they were about to attend. I would have been amused if the delegates involved had argued that they were already sufficiently empowered and chosen not to read it!

At the beginning of the day

I've never been terribly keen on some of the more traditional introductions and ice-breaker approaches to training – the 'Let's think of five interesting things to do with a pickled egg' routine, or the 'Let's all run around bursting balloons!' manoeuvre. I 'm always left pondering: 'Why on earth am I doing this?' 'What's the point?' And worse still I'm also usually left thinking, 'I feel a complete idiot doing this!' which does nothing for the relationship between trainer and learner particularly at this early stage. All groups quite rightly have in their minds 'What's in this for me?'

Telling a short story (approximately 30 seconds) can be a far more gentle ice-breaker, as it helps to relax both you and your group members. It helps to develop an atmosphere of mutual trust and respect and it's also a good way of gaining the group's attention in an innovative way.

By telling an appropriate story skilfully at the beginning of the day, you are encouraging the group into a positive frame of mind which sets the tone for the rest of the time that you're together.

In addition, if you find that the story has had a particularly good effect, you can recall it later in the day by saying, 'Do you remember the story I told you this morning about … well, this is another example of that …' or you can refer back to it for your conclusion.

Why is storytelling a more gentle and inviting method of introduction? Looking at it from a group member's point of view, the beauty of *your* telling a story at this part of the day is that any inherent risk is seen as being taken by you and not by them. I always find it surprising, when people express their feelings to me, how vulnerable they feel at this part of the day. And I find that they will go along with the idea of storytelling, sometimes almost out of relief as much as anything else, when they realize that they're not going to be involved in any activities that will make them look silly.

But now let's look at the scenario from your point of view. Telling a story so early in the proceedings *can* be risky particularly if you haven't done it before. Do make sure, if you're going to do this, that the story is appropriate, natural and enhances your rapport with the group.

I've seen some spectacularly unfunny introductions being told like a contrived 'Best Man joke', delivered in a very stilted and scripted style, and when it falls flat it can ruin your rapport with the group and it will probably take you the rest of the day to win it back. Remember that whatever you do now is seen by the group as setting the tone for the day.

At this point of the day it's best to tell a story from your own experience, so that you show your human face to the group, and establish trust and rapport. Do include humour, but remember that audiences are very astute, and will soon pick up that your 'A funny thing happened to me ...' tale did not really happen to *you* at all, but was adapted from your *100 Good Jokes for Trainers to Tell* book. If you're not comfortable with joke telling – don't!

On the other side of the coin, this doesn't necessarily mean you have to bore the audience to death with the 'Let me tell you a bit about myself' routine, where the presenter takes 20 minutes (or longer) to tell us the unabridged story of their life, and how they've worked for every blue-chip company you've ever heard of – and probably a few more besides.

I agree that you have to establish your credibility, but this is not an excuse for making a saga out of it. Nobody is really that interested in dry monologue, and as probably a large majority of the content won't be heard, much less believed, it doesn't do a lot for the credibility stakes.

A colleague of mine, having had a horrendous start to her own day, but determined to see the positive side, began a meeting with her staff with these words:

> ... Well, let me tell you what's happened to me so far today: first of all I managed to lock myself out of my car, then I found when I finally got to work that I couldn't get into the conference room because nobody knew where the key was, and the caretaker was on a fortnight's holiday. The bulb in the overhead projector has blown up, and apparently we don't have another and when I went to the toilet just now I broke the zip on my skirt ... any questions?

This introductory monologue was greeted with hilarious but sympathetic laughter from the team and created a spirit of 'things can only get better'. She carried this tale off well, because she did it in a self-deprecating but confident way that elicited support.

Compare that with the woman who started a speech on time management and personal organization with this story:

> Now normally I have some acetates with me to illustrate this talk. But I came by train to the conference today, and you'll never guess what happened when I was on the train. Yes, somebody stole my briefcase and in it were all the acetates and handouts that I was going to use tonight ...

Oh ... yes? We've all heard *that* one before. There must be more thieves going round this country trying to sell second-hand acetates and hand-outs than there are those dealing in drugs! – another story that was not believed. And particularly considering the topic of her talk, the irony of this opening story although it appeared to be lost on her, was certainly not lost on many of her audience and it did nothing to build trust or cred-ibility.

My personal feeling is that it's best to tell, rather than read a story at this part of the day. Bear in mind how important eye contact is in building rela-tionships with groups and how much of that is lost if you are reading from a book or script.

There is nothing wrong with telling other people's tales, but I have always worked on the principle of honesty as far as that is concerned. For one reason, I think it's only ethical to credit someone else for their story, and secondly, if you put across an incident as being your own when it wasn't, you won't have the necessary conviction to persuade your audi-ence and some of its original power will be lost.

A story can also be used to introduce the topic(s) of the day in a dyna-mic and memorable way. For example, I have used 'The Meaning of my Communication', p. 78, to introduce a seminar on communication skills and I conclude the story by saying, 'I just want to make sure we are all talk-ing about the same thing ...'

During the day

You can tell stories, analogies or introduce metaphors at any point during the proceedings where you need to inject colour, emotion, or humour, change the pace of the proceedings or to encourage those taking part to see concepts with more clarity.

You make the decision as to whether to read or tell a story in your own words. And if you don't feel confident in this skill (yet!), there is nothing to stop you playing an audio-cassette tape of a story, showing a video or even asking the group to read a story on their own. Bear in mind though, with this latter idea, that one of the main joys of storytelling lies in the sharing of information, thoughts and feelings. As Betty Rosen (1988) says 'Print is essentially solitary and ... people respond to company and imme-diacy.'

You can use a story as a powerful 'meta-message' during a seminar. '*Meta*' is Greek for 'hovering above' and really means that you are telling a story within a story. I ran a course for a small group of young managers in Winchester a couple of years ago and the majority of the members were very industrious and enthusiastic to learn. However, there was one indi-vidual who, for whatever reason, did not fit in with the rest. He did not have the same enthusiasm or commitment as the rest and he always managed to be late back from breaks and lunch. Now I hate going into my 'critical parent' mode of – 'And where do you think *you've* been?' – but we were fast approaching that stage.

On this occasion he had arrived back late from a break, and our group had already started talking about communication and the importance of congruence between verbal and non-verbal language. Just at the point that he returned to his seat, another member of the group said, 'Could you give us an example of congruent communication?'

> Well, let's see,' I said, 'let's imagine that you had a member of staff who had a problem with time keeping. To ensure that you got the point across that you weren't kidding, you would make sure that your body language matched your words, which might be … *time keeping is important here, and I really need you to* (looking straight at the errant delegate) *be back at work on time.*

Nobody else noticed or made a comment on what had happened, and even though nothing had been said directly to him that young man was never late again. This is a powerful way of getting a message across without alienating yourself from the individual, or changing your tone to that of the critical parent.

And, of course, meta-messages are not only used for corrective measures as in the above example: you can just as skilfully weave in inspirational or motivational messages to your stories . You can tell stories about people *succeeding against the odds, finding the learning easy* or *becoming a successful manager* in the same subtle way.

As a case study

I was running a course on building working relationships with a group of managers at a large medical company in the north of England. At the 'after lunch' spot, I read aloud the old folk tale 'The Enormous Turnip', p. 90, and then said, 'What relevance do you think this has to our topic today?' I offered them a copy of the script to study, and I expected that they might chat for a couple of minutes, and drag one or two points out from the story. But I was wrong!

Working in two groups, the members discussed, analysed and even argued about the content of the story for around 45 minutes and then reported back their findings, which I put up on the flip chart. These were the learning points that they identified:

- It takes a team effort to achieve the task.
- No matter how small a contribution a team member makes – it still counts!

- Don't make judgements about members of the team based on the opinions of others.
- Have courage in your own convictions.
- Adopt assertive behaviour when challenged by others.
- Involving the team is more productive than doing things on your own.
- Use different influencing style with different members of the team.
- Use appropriate language with different members of the team.
- Encourage, not bully, people to help.
- Give an incentive for each team member to do the task.
- Discuss the task with your team to get their ideas.
- Is there a priority 'pecking order' – could the farmer have gone straight to the mouse for help?
- Be aware of the size of the task and don't let it get out of hand.
- Identify the 'right' time to do the task – the turnip might have gone off by the time they had pulled it up!
- Share rewards among the team involved in the task.
- Give credit where credit's due!
- Who was the real team leader – was there an emergent leader?
- Don't dwell on the problem – focus on the solution.
- Be specific in your instructions. The farmer said, 'Grow, turnip grow' but didn't say when to stop!
- Be aware of the power of affirmations!

I was delighted with the enthusiasm, intelligence and obvious enjoyment that both groups showed in tackling the analysis of the story. They discovered learning points hidden in the style, the format and language of that story that *I* hadn't noticed!

This is another reason for not being prescriptive in deciding the moral of a story (see Chapter 2). I would encourage groups to get as much out of a story as they can; your role as facilitator is to ensure clarity in their thinking and to guide them back onto the track, if you think it necessary.

And for those of you who might be thinking 'Ah yes, this is all right for intelligent, senior managers', I have to tell you that on this particular occasion, the greatest advocate of this exercise was a security manager in his mid-50s, who had a reputation in the group for being a very autocratic, 'take no prisoners' sort of a chap who had, up to this point, spent most of the time irritating his colleagues.

He reported to me privately afterwards that the story had 'made him think'. It didn't change his life – that would have been too bold a claim – but if it even 'made him think' I consider that to be a worthwhile exercise!

Betty Rosen, in working with children, identified a similar phenomenon:

> Even before telling the story, I knew that the level of achievement of the pupils' responses would be high in both vision and language ... What I did not anticipate was the amount of thinking which gathered around the edges of what I had planned and which was revealed in quantities of spontaneous talk: about the origins of the stories etc ...
>
> (Rosen, 1988)

After this group's analysis of the story, the points on the flip chart then led us into a more work-related and conventional discussion in which we considered 'Which of these things do we currently do in our organization?' and also 'How might we encourage more of these positive points that we gleaned from the story?'

In addition to all the learning we derived from the tale, it gave us the added bonus of being a wonderful 'anchor' for the rest of the day, with many good-humoured jokes and comments like, 'That problem in our department was like ... pulling up the turnip!' and 'We need help ... somebody call the mouse!'

To illustrate a difficult concept

If you cast your mind back to Chapter 1, you'll remember that this was one of the key roles played by the original storytellers in the Middle Ages, and it's just as powerful a tool these days. By using stories, you are actually encouraging your learners to assimilate complex knowledge in an innovative way, and encouraging them to use the right side of their brains in a more creative learning process.

Some years ago I was working with a group of managers from a large printing company in the south of England who were trying to grasp the concepts of motivation behind communication and that 'every behaviour has a positive intention'. Although I had all the relevant hand-outs and the notes and the acetates, the theories didn't seem to be sinking in.

I said, 'Let me give you an example ... ' and I told them the tale of the young dyslexic woman: 'There's no Such thing as a "Difficult Delegate"', p. 102, where the woman's seemingly aggressive behaviour was simply a defence mechanism for stronger emotions that were going on underneath the surface of the iceberg. I then asked the question, 'Her behaviour had a positive intention, but for whom?' Of course, the answer is 'Herself'. It certainly wasn't seen as positive to *me* at that time. Not only did the story make the theory much clearer, but the group all started joining in then with their own examples of where they had met similar aggression, only to discover later that there were underlying reasons for it.

I normally end that tale with the 'tongue-in-cheek' warning, 'Now this doesn't mean that the next time you meet someone who is behaving aggressively you can dash up to them and say, "I know your problem; you're dyslexic aren't you? I've been on a training course ..."'

Nathan and Karin Harter (1993), working on a training course called 'conflict management' at a college in Indiana, USA in 1993, rediscovered by chance some of the old Aesop Fables, and realized how relevant they were to the concepts they were trying to get across to their students:

> A lion and a boar were fighting over a watering hole when they noticed a vulture perched nearby. 'Better to share the water,' they agreed, 'than to feed the likes of him'
>
> (Hanford, 1954)

They used this tale and others as case studies for discussion, as a way of illustrating the underlying models and concepts of conflict and to encourage learning. They were amazed with the success of the tales, but then said, 'Why are we so surprised? This is no real innovation, since the fables have been used repeatedly for this very purpose!'

It isn't only abstract concepts that can be illustrated with story. As described in Chapter 2, other experiments have been carried out on the power of story, where complex subjects such as electricity have been illustrated using story, analogy and metaphor, and when tested, the students who had been taught in this way had learned significantly more than students taught in a traditional way.

Albert Einstein – so the story goes – could only develop the theoretical equations for his theory of relativity after he had imagined the concept visually; he dreamed up a personal story of himself riding beams of light, surveying things below him, and wondering how observers from other points might view the same things.

As a challenge for your group

At its simplest level, you could use this technique by saying, 'Does anyone have a story that would illustrate that point?' to encourage individuals to tell their own personal anecdotes.

As mentioned in Chapter 2, metaphorical questions such as – 'If your company were a car, what would it be?', 'If your boss were a piece of fruit, what would she be?' – can be challenging and fun. This process links one concept with a seemingly unrelated one to give a different perspective.

In addition to my home-made cards mentioned in the previous chapter, I sometimes use a wonderful set of playing cards designed by American Roger von Oech called 'The Creative Whack Pack'! Each card – as well as having an appropriate story on it – poses such questions as:

How can you slay a sacred cow?   What rule or policy has been successful for you in the past, buy may be limiting you now?

Make a metaphor   What similarities does your idea have with cooking a meal? Conducting an orchestra? Raising a child?

Where do you hear the knock of opportunity?   How can you answer it?

Put a lion in your heart   What gives you the courage to act on your idea?

I encourage groups to 'take their pick' of the cards, and they serve as a novel and creative way of stimulating group discussion and encouraging 're-framing' or seeing things from a different point of view.

Or more challenging still is to invite your group to write a metaphorical story to illustrate their company's growth, where they see their department fitting into the whole organization, etc.

'The Pirate Ship' story, p. 134, is an example of where group members were asked to write their own stories to illustrate a 'challenging time' in the company. The test of its efficacy is whether the feelings, thoughts or beliefs of the individuals concerned changed in any way while they were writing or telling the story. In this case, it added a new dimension to what had been seen as a perennial problem.

It's interesting to consider that one of the traditional challenges to groups, 'role plays', are also stories but in another format. And yet how universally group members seem to hate them! I think the difference is partly because if an individual is involved in a role play, with very few exceptions, they see the activity as putting them at risk.

It's also interesting to note that, whereas with role play, the universal cry is always – 'Ah, yes, but it's not true to life' – the writing and telling of stories, which are actually far more fantastical than role plays, do not seem to attract this criticism. No one has ever said to me when they have heard a story, 'Ah yes, but it's not true to life'. Maybe the difference is that stories do not pretend to be anything other than fantasy and are therefore easier to accept.

After lunch

This is the time that all the trainers and managers I know refer to as 'the graveyard spot', and they traditionally think it is their solemn duty to ensure that delegates bounce up and down, run round the building and do just about anything to keep them awake. But consider that, while you might be keeping them awake, the effect that all this activity is having on their recently digested lunch.

Maybe we could learn something from our colleagues who work in kindergartens and nurseries. Are they so far removed from us? What do their students do after lunch? The most natural thing that their bodies could do – sit down quietly, maybe even have a little snooze, and let their bodies digest the food that they've just consumed.

And what better way to do all this *and* make the graveyard spot more productive than by telling a story! Make the most of the fact that your group will be in relaxed mode rather than fighting it, and be aware that this can be a most effective time for learning.

For an after lunch spot, however, I would suggest that you pick one longer tale (5–8 minutes in length). You're looking for a story that begins fairly quietly and calmly, to aid the relaxation and digestion processes, and then maybe later on energizes through humour, adventure, activity, etc.

If you can't find one suitable story that serves this purpose, you could of course use two (or even more if you have a receptive audience) – one quiet one followed by one more energetic one, or you might encourage the members of your group to join in a 'group storytelling' – this is a nice relaxed but still effective way of preparing them for the afternoon's activities. Consider this as a mental rather than physical workout before the afternoon begins.

Starting one story and then finishing it later

As discussed in Chapter 2, our brains quite naturally seek out pattern, completion and wholeness – or a gestalt. Because of this phenomenon, we find 'unfinished' conversations, jokes, jingles or indeed stories intriguing and sometimes infuriating!

The storyteller can utilize this knowledge in a positive way. Starting one story and then finishing it later is a useful technique that, once mastered, can maintain interest and involvement for a longer time. If you've set the scene sufficiently well, you will find your audience 'hooked' to know what happened next. If you remember, we said in Chapter 1 that the main focus of a story is the plot and – what happens next! By doing this, you maintain the levels of learning for a longer period of time. I use a lot of my stories in this way. 'Did I Tell you the One About …? ', p. 112, lends itself quite well to this treatment, as does 'There is no Such Thing as a "Difficult Delegate"', p. 102, and 'Fitness for the Purpose', p. 152.

One of my favourites for telling in instalments is the story of the man in 'The Wedgwood China Shop', p. 132. The story will normally be part of a discussion on stereotyping and the dangers of making assumptions. I set the scene by describing to the group the shop and the 'reptilian' character who appeared. When I get halfway through the story, I stop and ask the question, 'What do you suppose was going through that man's mind?' The answers I am given tend to be either 'They're not going to buy anything' (the most positive scenario) or 'They're going to steal something!' (the most negative scenario).

As I find most groups can relate to this tale because something similar has usually happened to them, we then lead into a discussion on 'How does it make you feel to be treated in this way?' and draw out points like belittled, devalued, insulted, angry and so on.

The final point is to return to the end of the story. 'So – do you think we actually bought anything from this shop?' '*No*' is the universal answer.

And, of course, the moral of that tale, as I tell the group, is that not only have I never been back to that particular shop, but I have told all my friends about that incident, as well as countless numbers of learning groups and now of course – *you*! And you'll tell your friends and so it goes on. Never underestimate the 'ripple' effect of stories!

And don't worry if you forget to return to the original tale. If you've done your work well, and generated the interest, one of your audience will say, 'So what happened to the manager with the wooden leg?'

You can take lessons from the great comedians to acquire this skill – Billy Connolly, Victoria Wood, Tommy Cooper, Ronnie Corbett, Frankie Howerd – all are masters at the art of the long-winded story.

At the end of the day

Before I realized what a valuable tool storytelling was, I have to admit the endings of my training courses were, to say the least, frenetic. There would be some people still filling in evaluation sheets or action plans, some had stood up, packed up and were raring to leave, and some would be trying to bend my ear on a personal issue. I could never determine myself when the actual 'end' of the seminar was, and it always left me feeling exhausted. So, goodness knows how the delegates felt!

A short, hypnotic story is a good way to wind down and to relax both your audience and yourself, and to bring about a more definite 'end' to the day. Your choice of story should be as important as the one at the beginning, for this is the final impression that you are going to leave them with – of the day, the content of the day and *you*.

Remember also how receptive the brain can be in this relaxed state when you have triggered off the alpha brainwaves, mentioned in Chapter 2. The message or moral of your story may be directly going into the subconscious minds of your listeners, so make sure that it is a suitable message with a positive, inspirational or uplifting note. It's easy to fall into the trap of so many otherwise excellent speakers I have heard, who end their talk with: 'So, *don't* forget, if you have any *problems* ... *don't* hesitate to tell me ...'. Do you really want a statement, filled with all these negative words, to be the last thing that resonates in the minds of your audience?

I very often devise my own story for the end of the day, where I can weave in all the points that we've covered in a kind of summary, as well as creating a 'bridge' or a 'future pace' back into the work place. You can start this while some are still filling in action plans, in this way:

> 'I'm conscious that some of you are still writing ... and as you do that we realize that we're coming towards the end of our day together ... and it will soon be time to go back to our jobs in the office/the site/the factory floor/the shop ... and we can see ourselves going into work tomorrow ... in the same way that we always do, but it won't be quite the same because we're different people now ... we have all these new and wonderful skills of ... assertiveness/motivation, and all the new knowledge that we've acquired today ... and you may find that some people won't recognize you, or will want you to return to being who you were before ... and that's all right, because it's just that they haven't learned the things that you have ... yet ... and when they do they will be able to support you and help you ... in just the same way that you support and help them ...'

If you can't think of your own story, then one like 'The Prince and the Magician', p. 118, is an excellent way to conclude a day, particularly if you have been dealing with slightly contentious issues, ones relating to change, or new concepts, and where people may still be feeling anxious.

On a surface level, the part being taken in by the conscious mind, this story has a hypnotic and relaxing quality and at a deeper level, the part going directly into the unconscious mind, poses questions about truth and reality that are very personal and profound to each of us.

Other good stories to end the day are 'A Leader's Prayer', p. 148, which makes a good end-of-day story for a day on leadership, and 'The Prophet' by Kahlil Gibran, p. 122, which has a nice hypnotic quality and is an inspirational end to any day where learning has been an important factor.

I have found that the only drawback to ending your day in this way is that the group members become so relaxed that they don't want to go home! Because, if you have done this well, what you have done is to induce the alpha level brain waves, which as mentioned previously is a state of relaxed awareness, a form of trance in the listener, and when you finish your tale, they are still in that state.

Eileen Colwell (1980), master storyteller, says that the greatest tribute that can be paid to a story and the telling of it is the moment of silence that sometimes follows. And she tells us not to worry about this; it simply means that the listener has been lost in another world, and it takes a little time for them to return to the real world.

So, be aware of this; let your audiences have that interlude of coming back to the 'other' world gradually, and don't break this moment by leaping up, clapping your hands and shouting, 'Well! Time to get on ...'

You can achieve a 'punchier' end to your day by using short, dramatic tales, such as the mini-saga, 'What the Sleeping Beauty would have given her Right Arm for', p. 76. A colleague of mine, who is an expert on equal opportunities, ended her talk to a group of human resources (HR) managers with that one, and found that it proved an energetic and light-hearted end to what can sometimes be seen as a 'heavy topic', but was at the same time thought-provoking and inspirational.

Other similar 'quick ending' tales might be 'Leave Well Alone', p. 128, 'The Sun and the Wind', p. 108, 'All Those Buns!', p. 155, or 'The Horse on the Road', p. 130.

For evaluation of training

Tony Grasha (1990), investigating a naturalistic approach to learning, carried out an interesting experiment in which he encouraged his groups of undergraduate students to evaluate a recent training course they had just attended in terms of a metaphor which would summarize the words, feelings and images that they had generated. He found that their contributions, as well as being a valuable evaluation tool, also provided useful insights into students' perceptions of the teaching–learning process itself and what their needs and preferences were as learners. The type of results he obtained were as follows:

Ineffective classes	Effective classes
A bike without wheels; a train on a circular track going nowhere; foreign movie without the subtitles and the audience can't leave the theatre because the doors are locked.	Basic training survival course; point at which three streams form one big river; survival trip into the wilderness on foot; travellers taking a pleasant trip back to place where they were born; explorers in a new land.

The 'left-brain' trainers and managers among you will be thinking 'This is not objective evaluation' and, of course, you would be right. But Tony Grasha argues that using metaphor in this way can provide in some cases a much richer and deeper view of student behaviour than from traditional quantitative measurement techniques.

After the day

At the end of the day, particularly if you are planning a follow-up event, you can ask group members to read a story and analyse it in relation to the topic you have been covering – either individually or in groups – with a view to giving their feedback on the next day. Or you can ask group members to make up their own story or metaphor to illustrate a particular point, and either read it out or role-play it, whichever is most appropriate.

I think it would be unwise to introduce this type of technique without warning at the end of the day, unless you had been using story as a learning medium and your group had become accustomed to it. The sudden transition from the real world to the imaginary might be a bit hard for some to take!

CHAPTER 4

It's the Way you Tell them

GAINING RAPPORT WITH YOUR AUDIENCE

What is rapport? Language experts would tell us that the word is derived from the French verb *rapporter* to bring back, or to refer, and that in English we understand it to mean a communication or understanding between people. In a business sense, as trainers or managers, we think of it in terms of 'being on the same wavelength' as somebody, or 'talking the same language' and it's one of those mysterious things that we take for granted – until it isn't there!

Incorporating stories, metaphors and myths into our communication style can help to achieve and maintain rapport with learning groups or audiences more easily. In storytelling terms, to have rapport means that there is a seamless blend between the three essential elements – the story, the storyteller and the audience – and the responsibility of achieving this blend lies with the skills of the storyteller.

Once you've made the decision about the content of the story, what its message or learning points are and where and when to tell it (as discussed in previous chapters) the next big decision is – how will you tell the story? What subtleties of process will you use that will help you to establish and maintain rapport with your audience? To answer this question, you have to consider it in three stages:

1. *Decide what outcome you want from telling the story*
And make sure you think of this in positive terms, for example, 'I want the audience to look at me intently,' rather than 'I don't want them to look bored.' What specific behaviour do you want to see from your audience that will tell you that you have achieved your outcome? Do you want them to laugh, cry, look at you intently, take notes, look at the ceiling?

2. *Be alert enough to notice what response you are getting*
This is where it helps to tell rather than read a story, as you can maintain

eye contact more easily with your audience. Be aware of their physiology but be careful not to make judgements. Just because John is sprawled in his chair with his hands behind his head does not necessarily mean that he is bored. It simply means that *he is sprawled in his chair with his hands behind his head!* Now you know that if *you* were engrossed in listening to someone, you would sit up and lean forward slightly, with your arms folded in your lap, and because that is your experience you expect everyone else to do the same but they don't! If John's behaviour worries you check it out by asking non-threatening questions such as, 'You're frowning John, is there something you're unclear on?' but not judgemental statements such as, 'Well, you're obviously *bored!*'

3. *Be flexible in your behaviour*
If the story you are telling is not getting the response that you were expecting, be prepared to change your behaviour, and keep changing it until you get the response that you do want. In other words, you might make subtle changes to your voice, stance, gestures, posture or eye contact. You might decide to cut the story short, exaggerate it or involve your audience. With each change you make, monitor what response you get and check it out against your desired outcome.

Don't fall into the trap that many trainers and managers do when talking about the flexibility of their behaviour – 'Well, that's just me; take it or leave it … I can't change the way I am!' We can and do change our behaviour very skilfully many times during the day, both at work and at home. The question is one of motivation rather than of capability.

Although I encourage flexibility in storytelling, I would also encourage you not to make any sudden or incongruent changes, like developing a false accent, or bursting into song, as this is more likely to give people the uneasy feeling of manipulation rather than rapport.

WHAT STYLE OF STORY?

Your choice of story format will help you to maintain rapport with your group. For example, you might decide to include some or all of these:

- tell your own story or anecdote
- retell somebody else's that you have heard
- read straight from a text
- adapt a written or oral story to suit the audience

Your decision here depends a good deal on what outcome you want from telling the story; it also depends on the type of group you are working with and the culture of their organization. For example, some groups will lap up traditional fairy tales, finding them therapeutic as well as educational. Other, more 'macho' groups would be horrified at the thought, and would much prefer the stirring 'We survived in spite of everything!' type of personal anecdote. Picking up cues from individuals during the day will help you to make the right decision.

You may find that if you decide to read a text, you need to adapt some of the language to suit you and your audience, which is why it's always a good thing to read it through and rehearse it first. For example, words like 'gay', 'pulled' and even 'fairy', which were quite acceptable in Shakespeare's day, won't convey the same meaning to modern audiences and although humour is a wonderful part of storytelling, you want to make sure that your group is laughing in the right places.

On the other hand, I have heard some beautifully written folk tales ruined by *over*-adaptation. If you're choosing alternative language, make sure that as well as being appropriate for the culture of your audience, it still fits in with the general theme of the story.

USING THE TONE OF YOUR VOICE

Telling stories to adult groups, particularly in a business setting, does require a certain skill; the storyteller has to be able to adopt the most appropriate style of voice, and this will depend on the situation, the story and the audience.

Some people think that all storytelling has to be done using what psychologists refer to as a 'mother-ese' voice – where the tone is lilting, quiet, rather breathy and a few notes higher on the scale than normal – and whereas this might be acceptable in some settings, it does nothing for the relationship that you may have built up with your group of senior and very 'streetwise' managers! And don't think that this tendency is restricted purely to women. I have heard men use a similar voice which comes across as just as irritating!

The immediate effect of 'that voice' is to create an atmosphere of superior adult talking to inferior child and that's definitely not the relationship you are trying to create in a business context. The skill of adult storytelling lies in being able to recreate a *childlike* attitude in your audience, not *childish*. There's a difference.

The tone of your voice should be sufficiently melodic to generate involvement and interest in your audience, but not so 'sing-song' as to be a distraction from the plot. Remember that the purpose of telling the story is so that others can enjoy and learn from it. Some storytellers mistakenly feel that they have to create a completely different voice for every 'character' in the tale. I grew up on a very happy and enriching diet of *Winnie-the-*

Pooh (Milne, 1926) and similar stories, and I am often horrified to hear some retold versions of this classic, where the storyteller's characterization – although well-intentioned – is just too exaggerated, and actually detracts from the magic of the story.

'Hello Piglet,' said Pooh   *(deep, growly voice)*
'Hello Pooh,' said Piglet   *(high pitched, squeaky voice)*
'Oh look, Piglet, there's Eeyore,' said Pooh. 'Hello Eeyore.'   *(deep, growly voice)*
'Hello Pooh Bear; hello Piglet', said Eeyore.   *(slow, melancholy voice)*

(with apologies to A. A. Milne)

... one begins to dread the appearance of Rabbit, Tigger and Kanga, to say nothing of Christopher Robin!

Although it is good for any storyteller to develop their range of voice tones, which can only be done through practise, you should be aware that, particularly in adult storytelling, the variations of the range are more subtle than in children's storytelling. You should use your voice tones to help maintain the interest of the audience and to enhance the credibility of the content.

In order to adopt the 'right' tone of voice for your story, it is important to first adopt the right state of mind. As we know, the mind and body are all part of the same human system, and whatever you do to one will affect the other.

If you don't believe me, try out this simple exercise. You can do this on your own, but if you can work with a friend or partner, or as part of a group exercise, you can get some useful objective feedback:

1. First, think of a pleasant experience that you had recently. (You don't have to tell anybody what it was!)
2. Now, get a clear picture of that scene, see who was there, remember where you were, etc. Is the picture in colour or black and white? Is it moving or static?
3. When you've done that, remember any sounds associated with the picture. Was there anyone talking? Some background noise? Or maybe it was silent.
4. And finally, remember how it felt to be in that pleasant experience, and really relive the memory.
5. As you relive the sights, sounds and feelings of that experience, *count out loud from 1 to 10.*
6. Now, think of a time that made you irritated or angry. Repeat the stages above and then *count out loud from 1 to 10 again.*

Now I can't predict how your voice will sound, because everyone is unique, but the chances are that there will be a noticeable difference in the way your voice sounds – one might be loud, fast, and clearly pronounced while the other is slower, quieter and more melodic. Whatever the difference, it's quite a dramatic demonstration of how our thinking affects our vocal qualities.

Here are some pointers that will get you into the right frame of mind for telling your story:

- remember you are an adult talking to a group of adults
- the group is just as intelligent as you are
- think of the story as some information that you are sharing with your group
- focus on the reason why you are telling this tale
- ask yourself what response you want from your audience
- focus on the content, the plot of the story
- 'own' the story and make it part of you to ensure credibility

Your voice is housed by your body, so naturally any changes in your body posture – whether you are standing or sitting, moving or static – will have an impact on the quality of your voice, and you need to take this into consideration with the nature of the story and the outcome you want to achieve.

If you're rehearsing telling a story, do experiment with different physiology beforehand, using the first position/second position exercises described in Chapter 3 to imagine the response you might get from your audience. At the very least doing exercises like these might give you a few giggles, which in itself is another positive therapy!

Tension in the body is probably the number one killer of the voice. How many times have you stood up to address a group of 50 people, and heard, rather than the resonant tones you were expecting, this far-away squeak coming out of your mouth? Patsy Rodenburg (1992), in her excellent book, *The Right to Speak*, offers various exercises that we can use to release tension in our neck and shoulders, spine or knees, and to encourage better breathing and posture.

THE PACE OF YOUR VOICE

The pace of your voice will be dictated to some degree by the nature of the story you are telling, and the effect you want it to have on the listeners. An amusing anecdote will be better told in an up-tempo pace; a relaxing, inspirational or thought-provoking tale will be better told using a slower pace.

You can, of course, change pace during the course of the story. You might be telling a story that begins slowly and quietly and then builds up the interest and excitement in the audience by increasing the pace to a crescendo or you might start a story using a fast pace, then use your voice to gradually slow the pace down, and with it the emotions of your listeners.

Make sure that you don't allow nerves to make you rush a story. The faster you speak – particularly if you are retelling someone else' s tale – the more likely you are to trip up and stammer on your words, and this spoils the enjoyment for the listener.

If you know you have a natural tendency to speak quickly, then rehearse the piece s-l-o-w-l-y, remembering the effect that thoughts have on the voice. More deliberate and natural breathing from the diaphragm rather than the throat can also help you to relax, which in turn will slow your voice pace down.

The stresses you make with your voice are elements of storytelling whose importance should not be overlooked. Particularly if you are reading or retelling a written story, you will need to rehearse it a number of times, to make sure that you are including the right amount of emphasis on certain words so that the message is clear. For example, the message conveyed in the phrase, '*Everyone* should enjoy a good story' would be different to 'Everyone *should* enjoy a good story'.

As a storyteller, you should also be aware of the powerful effect that speech rhythms can have on the listener. Betty Rosen (1988), in her book, *And None of it was Nonsense*, talks of how she used to think of rhythm as just another literary device, but then began to see it as a natural function and a very powerful tool, which can actually encourage the release of emotion.

> Rhythmic speech. Sung, swaying speech. And the baby rocks in her cradle. The disturbed child rocks consolation into himself. The Jewish and Muslim sway and rock into conviction over the open scriptures.
>
> (Rosen, 1988)

It is the rhythm and the repetition in stories that give them their hypnotic quality, which is what brings about the very pleasant trance-like state in the listener that we call 'alpha' brainwaves. As already mentioned, this is the most conducive state for people to learn and to deal with change.

THE VOLUME OF YOUR VOICE

As with the pace of your voice, the level at which you tell your story should be consistent with the content and style, and will also be dictated by the number of people in your audience. Although popular thinking in some trainers and managers is that the louder you talk the more people will listen, the reverse is very often true. You can actually encourage more attentive listening by lowering the volume of your voice, as it creates an atmosphere of shared confidence with your group. Imagine that you were about to share some juicy gossip with them and see what effect this has!

On the other hand, raising the volume of your voice from time to time can be an extremely dramatic ploy, but be careful not to overdo it or do it too dramatically. One trainer who I encountered ruined her otherwise skilful storytelling by effecting such sudden and extreme changes in the volume of her voice that she frightened the group to death – and the inevitable giggling broke out among its members!

NON-VERBAL COMMUNICATION

As a trainer or manager, we all know the importance of non-verbal communication; psychologists tell us that up to 90 per cent of our communication is transmitted through our physiology rather than our words. As storytelling is probably a heightened form of communication, you must realize that your every move and gesture will be noted by your audience – maybe not consciously, but it will be noted nevertheless.

As one of the keys to successful storytelling is that of credibility, the most important thing that the storyteller has to consider in non-verbal communication is that of 'congruence', that is making sure that what you say is being backed up by what you do or how you appear.

For example, there would be no point saying to your group, 'Let me tell you a really sad story about that …' with a huge grin on your face. You would simply find that your group would look at your non-verbal behaviour and take no account of the supposed 'sad' story that followed. Equally, there would be little gain in saying 'I'm going to describe the exciting future that this company holds for you …' with a facial expression that indicated doom and gloom.

This is actually worse than not telling a story at all. Think how stories told in this way are going to be remembered and relayed to other people:

'Did you hear what she said about the future of the company?'
'Well, it sounded pretty positive.'
'Yes, but did you see her eyes? She didn't look at us once. I don't believe a word of it …'
'Come to think of it, she always talks like that … do you remember the redundancies we had last year? Well …'

BODY POSTURE

Being 'centred' is the natural position for your body. It is where the weight is distributed evenly throughout your body, and there is no tension in any one part. Finding the centred position for your body will have a positive effect on your breathing and your voice. To find your natural centre, stand with your feet slightly apart, fully on the ground, directly underneath the hips, make sure your knees are unlocked, the spine is allowed to stretch out, the arms are hanging loosely and the head is resting lightly on top of the spine. Keeping your feet on the floor, gently rock backwards and forwards. Your body will tell you when it is out of alignment; it will find and return to its own natural centre.

Being centred is not the same as being 'rooted' to the spot. I have noticed this in myself occasionally when I am working with a group. I might be so engrossed in talking or listening to them, that I lose sight of the fact that my body has become immobile, static and slumped. This might go unnoticed while I'm in listening mode, but it has a profoundly negative effect on the voice. The voice becomes immobile, static and slumped as well!

The easiest thing to do is, of course, to immediately change your body posture, stand up if you've been sitting, walk around the group, swing your arms, clap your hands or call for a coffee break and you will notice how your voice immediately takes on its interesting tone again. And don't worry that your audience will think this odd; the chances are that they will take this as an invitation to do the same thing!

You can develop flexibility in your own body posture by using the magic of metaphor on yourself. Just suppose, that the next time you were facing a group of people, you thought of yourself in these ways:

If I were a ballet dancer, how would I move? How would the group look to me?
If I were a policeman, how would I move? How would the group look to me?
If I were a giraffe, how would I move? How would the group look to me?

Planting thoughts like these in your mind can not only make a dramatic difference to your body movements and your voice, but can actually change the way you see the relationship between you and your audience. It stands to reason that if you view yourself as a policeman your audience assumes the role of criminals!

EYE CONTACT

Eye contact is particularly important for successful storytelling. If you are recounting one of your own or someone else's experiences with which you are well-versed, eye contact is no problem. As you tell the tale, keep 'sweeping' the whole of the room, to include everyone, so that they all feel involved.

Reading a story, of course, is more difficult. You have to acquire the skill of reading the text, looking up regularly to make sure your audience is still 'with you' and then looking back at the text again without losing your place. This is something which I have found improves with practice; the better acquainted you become with the tale, the less you have to rely on the script, or worry about whether you've missed a bit out.

GESTURES

The use of gestures in storytelling is what makes it cross over the great divide and become acting! And to what extent you want to act out your stories depends partly on what you think is appropriate in your particular setting, and partly how confident you feel in your own capabilities.

In adult storytelling, I think gestures should be underplayed rather than overplayed; like tone of voice, they are there to emphasize the words, not detract from them. Eileen Colwell (1980), says that storytelling should be restful to watch as well as to hear, and tells the charming tale of a visiting storyteller to her school, who in her rendition of an action-packed children's poem, acted every movement suggested in the poem, and became so exhausted that she had to be helped from the platform!

If gestures are used subtly and infrequently, then the more effective and noticeable each one becomes. For example, in the tale, 'The Prince and the Magician', p. 118, the only gesture I use is to emphasize the line '... he rolled back his sleeves ...'. As well as adding emphasis to one of the main points of the story, the gesture itself becomes a powerful 'anchor' for the group.

CREATING 'ANCHORS' FOR IMPACT

An anchor is simply another term for a link or an association between some sort of external cue and an internal thought or feeling. We can all remember the story of Pavlov's dogs, and how, when they heard a bell ring, they started to salivate. Pavlov had set up a conditioned response between the bell and the expectation of food.

People create their own natural anchors all the time, both in business and personal environments: how many times has a person walked into your training room, and said, 'Uh, oh, a video camera!' even if it's turned off and has nothing to do with your training!

Years ago I worked for a managing director whose greatest fame was that every time she was in a bad mood, she happened to be wearing a red blouse. The red blouse soon became a negative anchor for her staff, indicative of a difficult time ahead. They even started referring to them as 'red blouse days'.

Professional orators, politicians, entertainers and comedians, who are after all storytellers, also utilize anchors. Martin Luther King used his voice as a powerful anchor when he repeated the phrase 'I have a dream' to conjure up feelings of passion, optimism and hope in his audience. The British comedian, Tommy Cooper, only had to give us his unique, palms-down, hand movement together with the phrase, 'Just like that', in a particular tone of voice, and we would immediately start to laugh. He too had created an anchor, a response in his audience.

This naturally occurring process can be used to positive effect in the learning environment. The purpose for doing it is to 'ground' or solidify learning experiences, so that they have more impact and can be more easily assimilated and remembered. Every time you reintroduce the stimulus, you should get the same response, and the more you repeat it the greater the strength of the response.

This is why advertising slogans like 'A Mars a day …' immediately flags up the response, '… helps you work, rest and play'. Through repetition, the slogan has become a conditioned part of our thought processing. We don't even have to think about it consciously.

How many of you, wanting to energize yourself and your audience, have stood up, clapped your hands together and said, 'So … ' in a resonant voice, and been aware that the group members, by way of response, have had a little shuffle, sat up in their seats, stretched, yawned and straightened their papers. The intriguing thing is that, subsequently, every time you clap your hands, you will notice you get the same response from the audience. Through repetition, you have created an anchor.

Now, if you asked these people, 'Why do you all shuffle when I clap my hands?', the chances are that they wouldn't have the faintest idea why, or even that they were doing it. Much of this behaviour is at an unconscious level.

Anchors are stronger and will be remembered longer if they have been linked to some intense emotional feelings. In Chapter 2 we talked about how the limbic system is situated near to that part of the brain responsible for memory storage, which explains why we tend to remember information more easily if our emotions are involved. Hence, the reason why most people can remember where they were when Kennedy was shot, or when John Lennon was murdered. They have created a link in their minds between the two.

I am reminded of a training course I ran for a private health care company in this country. The group I was working with was made up of trainers and facilitators, and part of the course required them to give their own presentations on topics related to learning and motivation. One particular group member, becoming so inspired and passionate about her topic, went to the flip chart, where she had a wonderfully colourful drawing of a human brain, and said, '… And this shows us the *power* (thump on the flip chart) of the brain!' The whole group – including me – leapt a few inches in the air, but then broke into spontaneous, unanimous applause.

When we all met again some months later, I asked the group, out of curiosity, what were the things that had most stood out in their mind from the previous course. Without hesitation, they all replied, 'Val doing "the *power* of the brain"!' (You'll notice they didn't remember any of *my* pearls of wisdom …) She had created an anchor by associating the passion of her delivery with the physical thump on the flip chart!

The very act of telling a story in itself can become an anchor for the group. That opening line – 'Once upon a time …' is another. Your tone of voice, your body movements, where in the room you are and even the time of day when you are telling a story, will all have an impact.

For example, if you want to energize, inspire or entertain your audience, you would stand up and move about to tell the story, almost in a dramatic fashion. The group will soon come to associate the fact that your standing up and moving in a particular way means that they are going to hear an entertaining or thought-provoking anecdote.

If, on the other hand, you want the group to relax, ponder, reflect or generally wind down, then it would be more appropriate for you to sit down to tell your tale. And here again, the group will soon begin to associate this behaviour. One group with whom I work quite regularly now associate being told a story with the 'after lunch' spot, and it's quite amusing to see them return to the training room, snuggle themselves into their chairs and assume a relaxed mode – all without a word of direction from me!

You can also create what we call 'spatial' anchors – that is you make a link or an association between the story and a particular part of the room. For example, when dealing with the subject of controlling performance, I might carry out a dialogue between two imaginary members of a team. To do this, I would be standing in front of the group, and the dialogue would go in this way:

(first person, addressing imaginary second person)
'She's told me to tell you off, because you're always late for work …'

(moving two feet away and facing the imaginary 'first person')

(second person)
'And just who do you think *you* are, to talk to me like that?'

You will find that after a very short space of time, you will only have to move to that part of the room that represents either first person or second person, and ask an open question such as, 'Can you imagine what happened?' and the group will answer knowing which character you are referring to.

In this example, as well as the spatial anchor, I also use a slight change of voice to denote the difference between the two imaginary characters and the voice is another powerful way of creating an anchor. You might have a particular phrase that you use, a higher or lower tone, a little laugh, a change in pace or volume, that the group begins to associate with being told a story, anecdote or metaphor.

INVOLVING THE GROUP

The classic technique of the rhetorical question that we tend to associate with some children's storytelling, eg 'And *what* do you think he found there, children?' is intended primarily to produce an effect, rather than to elicit an answer. The technique can be powerful but also rather risky as one teacher, telling a tale to a group of small children, found to her cost:

'He looked into the garden and *what* do you think he saw?'
'An elephant,' answers a boy confidently.
'No dear', says the storyteller kindly, 'it was only a small garden.'
'It was only a small elephant,' says the boy firmly.

But rhetorical questions – if used subtly – can be a valuable tool in adult storytelling. Contrast the previous example with the way in which I tell the tale of psychologist Elton Mayo who, in the 1920s, conducted experiments at the now famous Hawthorne electrical works in the United States to test the effects of lighting on levels of production.

'So, Elton Mayo and his associates started off the experiment by going round the factory turning all the lights up. If you were doing this, what effect would you expect this to have on production?'
'*Production went up.*'
'Exactly. And you'd be quite right. So, Elton Mayo was patting himself on the back and saying what a significant finding this was. Just out of curiosity more than anything, he decided he would turn the lights down to see

what happened. What effect would you expect *this* to have on production?'
'*You would expect production to go down.*'
'You would wouldn't you … and so did Elton Mayo. To his amazement, quite the opposite happened. Production still went up. In fact, he found that *whatever* he did with the lighting, *production still went up*. Well, Mayo and his colleagues were intrigued with this result, and so they asked some of these women workers who had taken part in the experiment, 'Look, we don't understand what's happening. We turn the lights up, and production goes up; we turn the lights down, and production goes up. What's going on?' And what do you think these women answered …?'

… and so the dialogue goes on. Because the material that you are dealing with here is factual rather than fantasy, the rhetorical question can be used in a safer, lower-key, more conversational way. Your audience is more likely to know the answers, and even if they don't, you are unlikely to get impossible answers like 'an elephant'. Mind you, you never know!

Using a questioning technique like this can prove to be a very powerful medium. The more members of the group feel they are involved in helping you to tell the story, the more they feel an actual part of it; emotions become aroused and consequently the more interested they become in the outcome and the more they remember.

Because these are rhetorical questions, it doesn't really matter if no one in the group answers – you simply answer the question yourself! But using this type of questioning can provide you with an opportunity of praising and acknowledging your group for their answers. 'Spot on!', 'Absolutely right!', 'You've hit the nail on the head!' are the type of congratulatory phrases that I tend to use.

Equally, a rhetorical question doesn't involve putting your learners on the spot, unlike some of the more traditional questioning techniques that trainers and managers might use, for example, 'What effect would you expect this to have on production … Jim?', at which point Jim, who has been enjoying his own private reverie, jumps a couple of inches out of his chair, finds there are 20 pairs of eyes focused on him and turns a delightful shade of pink – and we all immediately know that *Jim has not been paying attention.*

I have seen some trainers and managers use this ploy and congratulate themselves on 'getting one over' on the chosen individual, which, of course, they have. But make no mistake, this is a form of manipulation, and even if *you* forget the incident, the poor soul who was at the receiving end won't and will find a way of *revenge*!

Your aim in storytelling is to create an enjoyable, positive experience for both yourself and your group. Through the skilful use of your voice and body, your aim is to enhance the rapport between you, to build a bond and to encourage positive communication and learning. As Nancy Mellon says:

> The process of storytelling itself, through voice, gesture and good will and through the fonts of wisdom it opens, evokes from deep within a healthy state of creative adventure.
>
> (Mellon, 1992)

And where does that adventure lead us? Well, that's another story ...

PART TWO

Now Read On...

The Tales

HOW TO USE THE TALES

Let's say you're running a seminar with a group of senior managers on internal and external communication, or you're holding a department meeting to discuss the problems you have been having recently with communication within the team. You both want to find a suitable tale that will help you emphasize the point. First, you need to ask yourself two questions:

1. What aspect of communication do I want to highlight? For example, danger of making assumptions, customer care, appreciating different people's maps of the world, etc.
2. In what format do I want to use this tale? For example, as a basis for discussion, for an opener to a training course, etc.

Having decided on your purpose, you then:

- look down the matrix of the tales (Figure 1, pp. 70–71), to see which best covers the areas you want to include, eg 'communication' and 'customer care'
- flick through the tales, looking at the 'Introduction', 'Moral' and 'Reflection' parts of each of one, to find out what format I have used them in, eg as a case study, opener for a course, etc and which message most closely matches the point you want to illustrate.

In the best storytelling traditions, do feel free to adapt the tales, add your own insights, or elaborate when you tell them to your audience. This is what will bring them to life!

In terms of the layout for the tales, I didn't think I could do any better than to follow the format that Aesop used for his original Fables, so you will find that with each tale, I have used the following structure:

Introduction   – the origins of the story, how and where I have used it, eg as an 'opener' or 'closer', as a case study, etc

The tale   – the text

Moral   – the learning point or message of the story ,

Reflection   – in what learning situations this story might be used, eg to illustrate a point on communication, motivation or customer care

As mentioned in Part One of the book, there is always the possibility – taking into account the varying circumstances you find yourself in, the different stories, metaphors or myths that you choose to tell, and the way in which you tell them – that people will glean their own personal message from the tales, and of course, that message may be different to the one which you intended.

What's wrong with that, you might ask, so long as they glean something? Well, that depends largely on you as the storyteller, being clear as to what purpose you want the story to serve, and how important you think it is in terms of that purpose, that your audience receives the same message that you intended.

So, it wouldn't be right for me to take a prescriptive view in terms of what the message of each tale is and where and when each tale should be used. But I have given you my own suggestions and a number of options as to where I have found each tale seems to fit best in a learning context.

If you are reading the story to a group, you can then make the decision as to where you think a tale might be most useful, and also whether to divulge the 'moral' of the tale, or leave it to the group to form their own interpretations.

The primary areas of learning covered by the tales are:

- Communication
- Motivation
- Learning
- Delegation
- Goal setting
- Success not failure
- Leadership and teambuilding
- Influencing
- Negotiation

- 'Re-framing' or seeing things another way
- Inspiration
- Appreciating different people's 'maps of the world'
- Recruitment/appraisal
- Problem solving
- Humour
- Self-esteem
- Creativity
- Danger of making assumptions
- Customer care
- Managing diversity
- Empowerment
- Dealing with change
- Assertiveness

Each tale lasts no longer than approximately ten minutes in telling, and some are as short as 30 seconds. I have found working with adult audiences in business, that ten minutes seems to be around the threshold time, before they start to come out of their own fantasy world, and display withdrawal symptoms from such important things as mobile phones, deadlines and strategic thinking.

	Communication	Motivation	Learning	Delegation	Goal setting	Success/failure	Leadership/teams
1. '… And I'm not Joking!'	●						
2. The Tube of Toothpaste					●		
3. What the Sleeping Beauty would have given her Right Arm for							
4. The Meaning of my Communication	●						
5. Percy the Pot		●				●	
6. Sophie Learns a Lesson	●		●				
7. The Cookery Book Game			●				●
8. If in Doubt – Delegate!	●	●		●			●
9. Our Deepest Fear							
10. The Enormous Turnip					●		●
11. Memorandum			●				
12. Mother and the Knife Grinder	●						
13. The Moth and the Star					●	●	
14. Waste Paper		●	●				●
15. Keeping Body and Soul Together		●				●	●
16. 'There is no Such Thing as a Difficult Delegate'			●				
17. Alice Meets the Cheshire Cat		●			●		●
18. Setting the World on Fire		●			●		●
19. The Sun and the Wind							●
20. Autobiography in Five Short Chapters					●		
21. 'Did I Tell you the One about…?'	●						
22. The Ball of Wool		●			●	●	
23. The Project						●	
24. The Prince and the Magician				●			
25. Giant Steps						●	
26. The Prophet	●		●				
27. The Professionals		●				●	
28. The Miller, his Son and their Donkey							
29. Leave Well Alone			●			●	●
30. The Horse on the Road					●	●	●
31. The Wedgwood China Shop	●						
32. The Pirate Ship		●			●	●	●
33. Lessons from the Geese		●					●
34. The 'Correct' Procedure							
35. John's Tale						●	
36. Role Play			●			●	
37. How the Waters Changed			●				
38. Rodney's Tale			●			●	
39. A Leader's Prayer							●
40. 'Just a Bod'							●
41. Fitness for the Purpose						●	
42. All Those Buns!							
43. Six Honest Serving-Men	●		●				
44. Houdini and the Locked Door		●			●		
45. Revolution in your Mind							
46. The Tortoise and the Hare revisited						●	
47. 'Thank you for the Smile'							
48. The Parable of the Sower and the Seed			●				
49. Say what you Mean and Mean what you Say	●						
50. Atlas' Tale		●				●	

Figure 1 *How to use the tales*

Influencing	Negotiation	Re-framing	Inspiration	Maps of the world	Recruitment/appraisal	Problem solving	Humour	Self-esteem	Creativity	Making assumptions	Customer care	Managing diversity	Empowerment	Dealing with change	Assertiveness
●		●					●		●						
						●									
		●							●			●	●		●
				●						●	●				
		●				●	●								
●						●							●	●	
●															
●			●		●			●				●			●
●						●						●			
					●	●	●		●						
							●			●					
			●					●	●						
													●		
		●	●						●						●
●	●	●		●					●						
			●			●							●		
●	●														●
		●				●		●	●						●
●				●							●				
		●	●			●									
●	●	●		●		●									
		●	●						●						
			●					●					●	●	●
			●					●							●
			●					●							●
		●				●	●	●							●
											●		●	●	
						●							●		
							●			●	●				
													●		
			●			●									
						●		●					●	●	
		●	●					●							
		●	●	●						●				●	
		●	●												
		●	●			●									
				●	●				●						
		●					●	●							●
		●					●		●				●	●	
						●					●				
		●						●							
		●							●				●	●	
		●	●					●							●
		●	●	●					●						
			●											●	
							●	●							
		●	●											●	

1

INTRODUCTION

This is an account of one of those situations – and we've all experienced them – where we become preoccupied with our own sense of seriousness, and forget to see the funnier, and very often more positive side of life. I use this story to illustrate how one can use humour in a positive way, to diffuse anger and stress.

THE TALE

'... And I'm Not Joking

A few years ago, when my husband and I lived in a suburb of Leeds, our house was situated right on the corner of a main road, and as motorists were not allowed to park on the road itself, we were plagued by people leaving their cars outside our house. This made it very difficult for us to negotiate around them and pull into our own driveway.

One day, returning home from yet another delightful day at the office, my husband, having had to perform the by now all too familiar manoeuvres with the car, stormed into the house.

'That's *it*,' he shrieked, 'I've had enough!'

'Had enough of what, dear?' I enquired, calmly, looking up from the evening newspaper.

'That car is parked outside our house again ... and it's the same one every time. Well, I'm sick of it. *I'm going to teach him a lesson*.'

This last ominous remark was uttered grimly as he ran upstairs, taking the steps two at a time.

I remained downstairs, reading and pondering. What was he going to do? Discover some sort of weapon and challenge the driver to a duel? Seek out his Swiss army penknife ('You never know when you might need it ...') with which to scratch obscenities down the side of the car?

My mind was just going into overdrive considering the possible alternatives, when he returned a few minutes later, looking triumphant, and proffering an outstretched hand.

'There,' he said, with a satisfied air, 'I'm going to stick this note on his windscreen ...what do you think?'

Brought down to earth somewhat in the light of my recent thoughts, I dutifully read the hand-written note, which was made up of predictably tough commands, such as:

DO NOT PARK YOUR CAR HERE

and sinister threats ...

I WILL HAVE NO ALTERNATIVE ...

all of which was underlined at least five times for added impact.

'Very good,' I said, 'that should do the trick'.

As my husband was turning to leave by the kitchen door, with all the demeanour of a man with a mission to accomplish, I added, 'Just one ... small ... suggestion ...'

'What?' he asked, annoyed to have been stopped mid-tracks.

'Do you think it maybe loses *some* of its authority ... the fact that it's been written on a child's "Kermit the Frog" Muppet message pad ...?'

MORAL

The tale serves to illustrate how, in becoming so engrossed in a 'serious' topic, we often lose the ability to step back and view things from a more global – and very often more humorous – perspective. Goethe was quoted as saying:

'The maturity of a human being is to return to the seriousness of the child at play.'

We should aspire to being able to adopt dual perspectives – being able to take play seriously, and take life playfully.

REFLECTION

Communication
Re-framing
Humour
Influencing
Creativity

2

INTRODUCTION

*Trainer colleagues have very often said to me 'It's all right for you to use anec-
dotes. Things happen to you'. I use this story to show that I do not have exclu-
sive rights to peculiar happenings. The things to which my colleagues refer do
actually happen to all of us, but are not always seen as important or significant
or indeed even remembered. One thing that I have come to appreciate as a trainer,
is that in every situation there is the potential for learning.*

THE TALE

The Tube of Toothpaste

In the small village where I have lived for several years now, life revolves
around the village general store. This is the sort of shop that sells, orga-
nizes and communicates everything from shoe polish and stamps to
brain surgery and arranged marriages (but, of course, that's only on the
first Wednesday of the month!).

I had popped into the shop one day for a bottle of milk and as I waited
to be served, I noticed a little girl in front of me – she couldn't have been
more than six or seven – who had obviously been sent by mother on an
important errand.

When it came to her turn she gave Gary, the friendly shopkeeper, her
apparently well-rehearsed line, 'Could I have a large tube of toothpaste,
please?'

'Certainly, love.' Gary scanned the shelves of the well-stocked shop
and held up a standard tube, about six inches long. 'There you are.'

The little girl looked thoughtfully at the toothpaste, then with a puzzled
expression asked, 'Is that large?'

MORAL

Good question! In order to set and achieve effective outcomes, we must all have some benchmark with which to compare – whether that be sizes of tubes of toothpaste or quarterly sales figures. Unless we have a clear notion in our heads of what our desired outcome looks, sounds or feels like, it is unlikely that we will achieve our goal.

REFLECTION

Goal setting
Problem solving

3

INTRODUCTION

This clever example of the 'mini-saga' – a poem of 50 words exactly – serves as a wonderful way of either beginning or ending any training seminar covering such areas as equal opportunities, assertiveness for women or managing diversity. I have found that it provides an acceptably light-hearted, tongue-in-cheek perspective on what can become quite a 'heavy' topic without causing offence to anyone.

THE TALE

What the Sleeping Beauty Would Have Given Her Right Arm For

This princess was different.
She was a brunette beauty with
a genius of a brain.
Refusing marriage, she
inherited all by primogenesis.
The country's economy
prospered under her rule.
When the handsome prince
came by on his white charger,
she bought it from him
and started her own racehorse business.

(Zoe Ellis, 1988)

MORAL

I believe there is a message for everyone in this tale, which is to encourage us all to avoid stereotyping. It also shakes us out of our complacency that we can always predict the outcome of any situation!

REFLECTION

Assertiveness
Managing diversity
Creativity
Empowerment
Re-framing

4

INTRODUCTION

This is a true story, which I find useful to tell as an introduction to any training in communication or interpersonal skills. This is just to make sure that before we start we are all talking about the same thing!

THE TALE

The Meaning of My Communication

Some time ago, I had gone into a large book shop in Leeds to buy a particular book on neuro-linguistic programming (NLP). This was in the days before NLP was terribly well known, and I wasn't surprised not to find hundreds of copies of it on the shelves. In fact, there weren't any copies of it on the shelves. I approached a youngish chap who was behind the counter, and, quoting the book title, asked whether it was in stock. He surveyed me, rather suspiciously.

'What's it's about?' he asked. This wasn't such a daft question as you might think, particularly if you had never heard of neuro-linguistic programming before. But I was stuck for an easy answer (and have been ever since incidentally, when asked for a definition of NLP in a nutshell).

'Well,' I said hesitantly, 'I suppose it's about … communication.'

'Aaaah …' he said, with a 'why didn't you say that before?' sort of look on his face. 'Follow me.'

He shot off with speed and enthusiasm down to the other end of the shop, with me in hot pursuit. Eventually, he stopped in front of a particular section of books, and started scouring the shelves confidently. I, not wanting to appear unhelpful, and always keen to build rapport with people, started obligingly scouring the shelves with him. After a while, however, I began to feel a little puzzled. I looked up at the section heading, and pulled the young man's sleeve.

'Excuse me,' I said politely, 'why are we looking at the "Computers" section?' He gave me a contemptuous stare.

'You said the book was about communication,' he answered.

'Oh, no, I'm sorry,' I said laughing, 'I meant … you know … *people* talking to each other – not machines!'

He surveyed me with disdain. 'I believe you want "Psychology", madam,' he said with a sneer.

I was tempted to say, 'Yes, don't we all,' but I managed to hold myself back … it would have ruined the rapport.

MORAL

The tale illustrates the dangers of making assumptions, firstly about communication itself, and secondly in expecting our 'own map of the world' to be the same as somebody else's.

For all our sophistication of computers, faxes, mobile phones, and now, God help us, the Internet, some of us are still in the Dark Ages when it comes to good, honest, face-to-face interaction with others.

REFLECTION

Communication
Danger of making assumptions
Appreciating different people's maps of the world
Customer care

5

INTRODUCTION

Every so often (some might say, too often) when the muse lands upon me, I feel inspired to write poetry. I made up this poem, partly just to entertain my niece, who had had a nasty accident, and ended up with a plaster cast 'pot' on her leg, and partly to encourage her to 're-frame' the situation, and see the pot as helping her to get better, rather than just being a very heavy and uncomfortable burden. She was delighted with the result, and insisted that I write the whole thing in rainbow coloured felt pens on the plaster – It took me hours – only to be informed by her the following week that she had been back to hospital and had the pot cut off! There's gratitude for you!

THE TALE

Percy the Pot

Percy the Pot doesn't say an awful lot
Doesn't shout and doesn't gripe
He's the strong and silent type

He's the type that you would call on
When you'd gone and slipped and fall-on
He's the sort you want around
When you're splattered on the ground

Percy the Pot says he knows he weighs a lot
And he's trying to lose some ounces
Just by doing bumps and bounces

But it's hard to lose weight faster
When you're made of heavy plaster
And you're tall enough to touch
From someone's toe to someone's crutch

Percy the Pot doesn't say an awful lot
He's not confident with talking
He just concentrates on walking

For walking is his forté
Even though he's not that sporté
And he makes sure bones get mended
While your leg remains unbended

So, it's three cheers for our Percy
He's the Hero of our time
The only Hero looking forward
To being cut off in his prime!

MORAL

The tale illustrates that not everything that seems unpleasant is bad for us … and equally that not everything that seems pleasant is good for us! If we can see difficult situations in a different, more positive way, it changes or 're-frames' the way that we feel, think and ultimately behave towards that situation.

REFLECTION

Problem solving
Re-framing
Success not failure
Motivation
Humour

6

INTRODUCTION

Most children are quite naturally tuned into observing the response they get from other people (particularly adults) and knowing whether it's the one they wanted. And they intuitively adapt their own behaviour according to the response they get. I use this tale to illustrate the point that, as we grow older, many of us seem to lose this skill of observing other people's behaviour, becoming instead more preoccupied with our own.

THE TALE

Sophie Learns a Lesson

My friend Viv's little girl, Sophie, was just two years old, not yet conversant with language, but very bright and rapidly beginning to find out the 'rules' of everyday living. Like all proud new mothers, Viv was encouraging her daughter to entertain a group of friends.

'Who's the boss in this house then?' she asked Sophie.

'Me!' shrieked Sophie, pointing to her chest, naturally to the delight of the assembled audience, who applauded and laughed.

Now, although Sophie could not fully understand the significance or the humour of what had just happened, she was sufficiently 'switched on' to register the reaction of her audience.

One can imagine the thought processes working.

'Hmm,' she thinks to herself, 'now when I do that, all my mother's friends laugh and smile and pat me on the head. I wonder what would happen if I did it again?'

And so the learning process begins ...

MORAL

One could argue that our 'intention' in communication counts for nothing, and that we should instead attach more importance to observing the response that our communication provokes, and asking ourselves whether this is the response we want. If it is, we can carry on using the same type of communication; if not, we can adapt our behaviour until we get the response we do want.

The meaning of my communication *is* the response I get.

REFLECTION

Learning
Communication
Influencing

7

INTRODUCTION

I came across this tale in Valerie Stewart's excellent book, The David Solution – How to Liberate your Organizations through Empowerment. *I'm sure we've all played what she calls 'the cookery book game' at some time in our lives. It's easy to kid ourselves into thinking that just because we've read the book, hired the 'guru', seen the video and picked up the latest catch-phrases, that we are automatically better people because of it. And it's also easy to be lulled into thinking that someone or something else has all the answers to our problems. (If you want to know why she calls it 'The Cookery Book Game – you'll have to read the book!)*

THE TALE

The Cookery Book Game

In the days when terms like organisation development and process consultancy were relatively new, one of the great gurus was Chris Argyris. (Still is, actually.) A smallish British firm decided that it had a need for some Organisational Development, whatever that was, and saved up its pennies to buy one whole day of Argyris's time. The entire board assembled to hear him speak.

Argyris took his seat and was silent. After a while one of the board members stood up and began describing their problems. Argyris remained silent.

Another board member then began to speak. And another, and another ... but still nothing from Argyris. Soon the flip chart had been covered with words and diagrams and everyone except Argyris was engaged in debate.

His silence continued over lunch. At three o'clock the Managing Director had finished an elaborate diagram of a current problem and Argyris stood up, went to the flip chart, and picked up the magic marker left by the MD. A hushed silence fell on the group.

Argyris capped the magic marker, and as he replaced it in its trough said:

'You know, if you don't put the caps back on these things, they dry up.'

And that was the last thing he said.

Valerie Stewart, 1990

MORAL

Here was a man that was not willing to go along with the game of dependency and disempowerment. His consultancy skill was in recognizing that this group of people already had all the resources they needed to effect change.

REFLECTION

Learning
Leadership and teambuilding
Problem solving
Empowerment
Dealing with change

8

INTRODUCTION

I sometimes wonder what we did before we had computers. They can save us so much time, can help us in creativity and resourcefulness, and help us in our learning. Some say they can teach us how to relate to other people. Some say they can take the place of other people! I am yet to be convinced on these two. I use this tale when specifically discussing the topic of delegation, but it also works well when talking more generally about leadership or getting the best out of people.

THE TALE

If in Doubt – Delegate!

I was hoping to do some work with a company who had just invested a large amount of money in some sophisticated computer software to enhance their sales performance. While being given a tour of the building, I was asked by the sales director if I would like to see this piece of software. 'Amazing capabilities,' said the chap enthusiastically.

'Certainly,' said I, always keen to show an interest.

I was duly introduced to the system, which was indeed highly sophisticated, and I 'Oooh'ed' and 'Aaah'ed' my way through, hopefully in the appropriate places.

I was just approaching the point where I was running out of superlatives to use, when my host exclaimed, 'And *this* is one of the best bits of the whole thing ...'

Intrigued, I perked up again, and leaned closer to the screen. He was pointing to a button which said 'Delegate'.

'What does that do?' I asked, hoping I was going to be wrong in my anticipation of his answer.

'Well,' he said excitedly, 'if I want to get rid of some really tedious work, I type it into the computer and then press 'Delegate' and it goes straight down the line to all of my sales team.

'And,' he continued, 'do you know the best bit? I don't even have to see them face-to-face to do it.'

86

I refrained from comment – this was a potential client after all – but consoled myself with the thought that, presumably, if the process was so easy, his sales team could just as easily 'delegate' the whole thing back to him. I do hope so …

MORAL

If you think human interaction is as easy as pushing a computer button, you do so at your peril.

REFLECTION

Communication
Delegation
Leadership and teambuilding
Motivation
Influencing

9

INTRODUCTION

Something that has shocked and saddened me over the years is just how many people appear to suffer from feelings of low self-esteem, and how the poor opinions people hold of themselves limit their success. This inspirational piece, Our Deepest Fear, *is an extract from a speech made by Nelson Mandela. I have used it on personal development and self-esteem seminars, and as part of appraisal training, to demonstrate that by having low self-esteem, you are not doing yourself, your colleagues or the world any favours.*

THE TALE

Our Deepest Fear

Our deepest fear is not that we are inadequate.
Our deepest fear is that we are powerful beyond measure
It is our Light, not our Darkness, that most frightens us.
We ask ourselves, who am I to be brilliant,
gorgeous, talented, fabulous?
Actually, who are you NOT to be?
You are a child of God. Your playing small
does not serve the World.
There is nothing enlightened about shrinking so that
other people won't feel insecure around you.
We were born to make manifest the glory of God
that is within us.
It is not just in some of us;
it is in everyone.
As we let our own Light shine, we unconsciously
give other people permission to do the same.
As we are liberated from our own fear,
our presence automatically liberates others.

(Nelson Mandela, 1992)
'Our Deepest Fear', from A Return to Love *by Marianne Williamson.*
Copyright © 1992 by Marianne Williamson.
Reprinted by permission of Harper Collins Publishers, Inc.
Portions reprinted from A Course in Miracles. *Copyright © 1975 by Foundation for Inner Peace, Inc. All chapter openings are from* A Course in Miracles.

MORAL

We should all remind ourselves from time to time of our strengths rather than focusing on our weaknesses and be proud to 'let our light shine through'.

REFLECTION

Influencing
Inspiration
Self-esteem
Managing diversity
Appraisal
Assertiveness

10

INTRODUCTION

This is a retold traditional folk tale which I have used very successfully as a case study on leadership, teambuilding and influencing skills training courses. (See Chapter 3 for more details.) It is what is known as a 'cumulative' tale, that is there are definite stages to the story, and in each stage characters and activities are added on. The result is a rhythm and a repetition which is hypnotic in quality, and helps to induce alpha brainwaves – the best level for learning and remembering.

THE TALE

The Enormous Turnip

Once upon a time, an old man planted a little turnip seed, and said, 'Grow, grow little turnip, grow sweet and strong!'
And sure enough, the turnip grew up sweet and strong – and big – and bigger – and ENORMOUS!

One day, the old man decided it was time to pull up the turnip. He pulled and pulled and tugged and tugged, but it would not shift. He called to the old woman, 'Old woman, come and help me pull up this turnip.'

The old woman got hold of the old man and the old man pulled the turnip, but to no avail. They still could not pull it up. So the old woman called to her granddaughter, 'Granddaughter,' she said, 'come and help us pull this turnip up.'

The granddaughter got hold of the old woman, the old woman got hold of the old man and the old man pulled the turnip. They tugged and heaved, but still the turnip did not move.

The granddaughter called to the black dog, 'Black dog, come and help us to pull this turnip up.'

The black dog got hold of the granddaughter, the granddaughter got hold of the old woman, the old woman got hold of the old man and the old man pulled the turnip. But no luck – the turnip remained just where it was.

The black dog called to the cat, 'Cat, come and help us pull this turnip up.'

The cat got hold of the black dog, the black dog got hold of the grand-daughter, the granddaughter got hold of the old woman, the old woman got hold of the old man and the old man pulled the turnip. But still they had no success.

'Well,' said the cat, as they all tried to get their breath back, 'the only thing left is to call the mouse.'

'The MOUSE?!' the others exclaimed, 'what good will he do ... he's so small!'

Nevertheless, the cat called the mouse, 'Mouse, will you come and help us pull this turnip up?'

The mouse got hold of the cat, the cat got hold of the black dog, the black dog got hold of the granddaughter, the granddaughter got hold of the old woman, the old woman got hold of the old man and the old man pulled the turnip.

'POP!' – out came the turnip at last.

And so that night they all enjoyed a delicious meal of turnip, and the mouse sat at the head of the table.

MORAL

The meek shall inherit the earth or possibly the turnip! Do you have any 'mice' in your team? If so, never underestimate them. It may be that their weight is just enough to tip the balance.

REFLECTION

Leadership and teambuilding
Managing diversity
Problem solving
Goal setting
Influencing

11

INTRODUCTION

I like this tale as it appeals to my sense of the ridiculous and the 'what might have been'. Who knows? It might be true! I use the tale as a light-hearted way of ending seminars on recruitment, psychometric testing, appraisal interviews, etc and it is one that actually seems to work just as well written as spoken.

THE TALE

Memorandum

To: Jesus, Son of Joseph, Carpenter's shop, Nazareth
From: Jordan Management Consultants, Jerusalem

It is our opinion that the 12 men you have picked to manage your new organization lack the background, educational and vocational aptitude for the type of enterprise you are undertaking. They do not have the team concept.

Simon Peter is emotionally unstable and given to fits of temper. Andrew has no qualities of leadership. The two brothers, James and John, place personal interests above company loyalty. Thomas demonstrates a questioning attitude that would tend to undermine morale.

We feel it our duty to tell you that Matthew has been blacklisted by the Greater Jerusalem Better Business Bureau. James, the son of Alphaeus, and Thaddaeus have radical leanings and both register high on the manic depressive scale.

One of the candidates, however, shows great potential. He is a man of ability and resourcefulness, has a keen business mind and contacts in high places. He is highly motivated and ambitious. We recommend Judas Iscariot as your controller and right-hand man.

We wish you every success in your new venture.

MORAL

If we can learn to combine science with common sense we will probably achieve miracles!

REFLECTION

Recruitment/appraisal interviewing
Delegation
Creativity
Problem solving
Humour

12

INTRODUCTION

My mother was a wonderful woman, very tall, slim and elegant and a profes-
sional businesswoman, who had a beautifully refined and eloquent speaking voice
– when she remembered! However, on occasions she would quite innocently, and
often with no idea of their significance, pick up inappropriate and rather crude
phrases or sayings – usually, I have to confess, gleaned from my sister or me –
which, when spoken in her best BBC voice, sounded somewhat incongruent to
say the least. 'Good Laaaawwd,' she would say, looking out of the window at the
rain, 'It's pissing it down again!' Once, when playing the word-game, Scrabble,
mother, whose turn it was, sat for a prolonged and tense silence before tri-
umphantly shouting 'Git!' to the surprise of the refined group of ladies who were
her guests. But mother was a great raconteur with a wicked sense of humour, and
used to tell this true tale – when she could control her own laughter – to point
out the danger of making assumptions.

THE TALE

Mother and the Knife Grinder

This tale goes back to the days – around 40 years ago – when in my home
town of Scarborough on the east coast it was a common sight to see
knife grinders roaming the streets, and to hear them shouting their wares.
'Knifes to grind … any knifes to grind …'

My mother was used to this practice, and was equally used to returning her standard response if the chap came knocking at the door. This
was because my father at that time had his own butchery business, where
among other things, they had all the equipment necessary for keeping
knives constantly sharp, so should any of mother's household utensils
become blunt, she would simply hand them over to father who would
arrange to have them sharpened.

'No thank-you,' was mother's standard reply to the knife grinder, 'that
won't be necessary', and then by way of explanation, 'my husband does
it all.'

One day, while at the local shops, my mother had noticed the knife
grinder on his rounds, and had made a mental note to expect a visit later

in the day. Sure enough, shortly after her return home, the doorbell rang.

Feeling somewhat irritated, as she was in the middle of cooking, mother went to answer the door. 'Yes?'

The anticipated tramp-like figure greeted her on the doorstep, mumbling what she took to be the usual sales pitch.

Without thinking, or even waiting for him to finish, she trotted out her standard line, 'No thank you, my husband does it all …'

Somewhat perturbed by the look she received as his response, she asked him, 'I'm sorry, *what* was it you said?'

The man replied, 'I said did you want any manure for the garden …?'

MORAL

This tale shows the potential dangers of making assumptions, firstly in thinking we know what people have said or are going to say, and secondly in thinking that we can judge people's characters or professions by how they appear. Appearances can be deceiving!

REFLECTION

Danger of making assumptions
Communication
Humour

13

INTRODUCTION

I first discovered the work of the American writer, James Thurber (1940) some 30 years ago, and grew up with such wonderful stories as The Secret Life of Walter Mitty, Many Moons *and* The Thirteen Clocks. *I think at that time I enjoyed Thurber's work purely on the basis of his being a marvellous storyteller, both for children and adults. Nowadays, I can appreciate the more profound messages that are very often hidden in the stories. I have used this tale, which is an extract from the book,* Fables for our Time, *to illustrate points on goal setting, having courage in your own convictions and also how our own dreams and aspirations may differ from other people's. Our worlds are not necessarily 'right' or 'wrong' – they're just different.*

THE TALE

The Moth and the Star

A young and impressionable moth once set his heart on a certain star. He told his mother about this and she counselled him to set his heart on a bridge lamp instead. 'Stars aren't the thing to hang around,' she said, 'lamps are the thing to hang around.' 'You get somewhere that way,' said the moth's father, 'you don't get anywhere chasing stars.' But the moth would not heed the words of either parent. Every evening at dusk when the star came out he would start flying toward it and every morning at dawn he would crawl back home worn out with his vain endeavour. One day his father said to him, 'You haven't burned a wing in months, boy, and it looks to me as if you were never going to. All your brothers have been badly burned flying around street lamps and all your sisters have been terribly singed flying around house lamps. Come on, now, get out of here and get yourself scorched! A big strapping moth like you without a mark on him!'

The moth left his father's house, but he would not fly around street lamps and he would not fly around house lamps. He went right on trying to reach the star, which was four and one-third light years, or twenty-five trillion miles, away. The moth thought it was just caught in the top branches of an elm. He never did reach the star, but he went right on trying, night after night, and when he was a very, very old moth he began to think that he really had reached the star and he went around saying so. This gave him a deep and lasting pleasure, and he lived to a great old age. His parents and his brothers and his sisters had all been burned to death when they were quite young.

MORAL

Who flies afar from the sphere of our sorrow is here today and here tomorrow.

REFLECTION

Goal setting
Appreciating different people's maps of the world
Success not failure
Self-esteem

14

INTRODUCTION

I have always thought that actually experiencing something for yourself is a better and more motivational way of learning than merely being told about it. And this true story is a good illustration of that. I have told this tale equally well to trainers to illustrate participative learning techniques, and to managers or supervisors to illustrate the concept of goal setting and motivation.

THE TALE

Waste Paper

I once observed a skilful trainer conducting a seminar on goal setting with a group of young managers.

'Stand there,' he said to the first volunteer, 'and your task is to throw as many screwed up pieces of this newspaper as you can into this waste-paper bin.'

Looking decidedly sheepish, the young man complied, and very slowly and suspiciously started rolling up the sheets of newspaper provided for him, and threw them into the bin. After a minute, the trainer intervened.

'Had enough?' he asked the by now confused delegate, who answered in the affirmative, grateful to return to his seat.

The trainer counted the number of balls of paper in the bin. He then addressed the second volunteer.

'Right, your task is to throw as many screwed up pieces of newspaper into this bin in one minute, and your target to beat is 21.'

The second manager, a woman, set about the prescribed task with determination, and achieved a final score of 29.

The trainer addressed the third volunteer.

'Right,' he said, 'you've seen what these others have achieved. What do you think you can do in the same time?'

'I can beat those two – no problem!' said the volunteer, rolling his sleeves up.

The third volunteer set about the same task, and managed to throw 33 pieces of newspaper into the bin.

'But that's not fair,' cried the first volunteer, 'you didn't give *me* the rules.'

'But that's not fair,' wailed the second volunteer, 'You didn't give me any choice.'

'It was perfectly fair, ' said the third, 'I knew what I had to do and when, and more to the point, I got a say in what target I thought I could meet. I set myself the highest target of all and I achieved it! '

MORAL

How many of us are asked to achieve a task without being involved or fully understanding 'the rules'? And what greater accomplishments might we make if allowed to set our own targets?

REFLECTION

Goal setting
Leadership/teambuilding
Empowerment
Learning
Motivation

15

INTRODUCTION

This tale is a great challenge to inertia and complacency; I have used it with all levels of management and staff within different types of organization to encourage them to see that there is another way to do things – and that that way can be extremely successful. I also encourage groups to compare Anita Roddick's philosophies of business with those of their own organization.

THE TALE

Keeping Body and Soul Together

I didn't know anything about business when I opened the first Body Shop in Brighton in 1976. The vocabulary of business was part of a language I did not speak. And I certainly had no ambitions to start a big international company. I didn't want to change the world; I just wanted to survive and be able to feed my kids. The extent of my business acumen went no further than the grim knowledge that I would have to take in £300 a week to stay open. But I did know how to trade.

I started with a kind of grace which clung to the notion that in business you didn't tell lies. I didn't think of myself as an entrepreneur. My motivation for going into the cosmetics business was irritation: I was annoyed by the fact that you couldn't buy small sizes of everyday cosmetics and angry with myself that I was always too intimidated to go back and exchange something if I didn't like it. I also recognised that a lot of the money I was paying for a product was being spent on fancy packaging which I didn't want. So I opened a small shop to sell a small range of cosmetics made from natural ingredients in five different sizes in the cheapest possible plastic containers.

I did not deliberately set out to buck the trend – how would I even know what the trend was? – but it turned out that my instinctive trading values were diametrically opposed to the business practices of the cosmetics industry in just about every area:

- They were prepared to sell false hopes and unattainable dreams; I was not. From the start, we explained to customers in simple language everyone could understand exactly what a product would do and what it wouldn't do.

- They sold through hype; I was so innocent I didn't even know what hype was.
- They thought packaging was important; I thought it was totally irrelevant. We happily filled old lemonade bottles with our products if a customer asked.
- They tested on animals; I was repulsed by the practice and made it clear that I would never sell a product that had been tested on animals.
- They spent millions on market research; we simply said to our customers, 'Tell us what you want and we will try and get it for you.'
- They had huge marketing departments; I never fully understood what marketing was.
- They had enormous advertising budgets; we have never spent a cent on advertising. At the beginning we couldn't afford it, and by the time we could afford it we had got to the point where I would be too embarrassed to do it.
- They talked about beauty products; I banished the word 'beauty'.
- They worshipped profits; we didn't. In all the time I have been in business we have never had a meeting to discuss profits – we wouldn't know how to do it.
- Finally, and most importantly, they thought it was not the business of business to get involved in wider issues, in the protection of the environment or involvement with the community; I thought there was nothing more important.

I honestly believe I would not have succeeded if I had been taught about business.

Kind permission is granted by Crown Publishers Inc. for the use of Body and Soul *by Anita Roddick.*

MORAL

There are times when ignorance is bliss!

REFLECTION

Motivation
Success not failure
Re-framing
Inspiration
Leadership and teambuilding
Creativity

16

INTRODUCTION

This seems to be a tale that everyone I have told it to (and there must have been hundreds!) can relate to, and it is particularly relevant for trainers or managers who have had to deal with the occasional 'difficult' member of staff. It is useful to remember that we all have choice in our behaviour.

THE TALE

'There is No Such Thing as a "Difficult Delegate"'

The trainers among you can no doubt imagine the scene that I am about to describe. I was running a course on influencing skills, with an established client, and I was using an old favourite of a questionnaire which I had used many times before. No one had ever experienced any difficulties with this. It was an easy questionnaire – or so my 'map of the world' dictated.

Suddenly and completely unexpectedly, a young woman at the back of the room started to behave – in my view – very irrationally.

'What stupid questions,' she said, firstly in a loud 'stage whisper' to her partner. 'What a waste of time. Why do we have to waste our time filling in these silly things?'

Now the sensitive trainers among you who are reading this will by now be breaking into an empathetic cold sweat! What do you do in the face of such an attack? Shout back? Ignore it? Try and rationalize? Enlist help from the other members of the group?

The most instinctive reaction is to attack – trainers are human after all – well, most of them!

'Don't be so stupid,' I was tempted to say. 'This is an easy questionnaire; a child could do it. No one else has had any difficulty ...'

You'll be pleased to know that I did not succumb to this retort. Instead, still with my professional smile intact, I went and sat down next to the young woman, who was still whining her complaints – but now louder – to anyone who would listen.

'How's it going?' I asked pleasantly, 'Is it making any more sense?'

She waited until her partners were occupied, and leaning towards me whispered, 'I'm dyslexic and I can't read these questions; my employer doesn't know, and if you tell him, I'm going to lose my job. Please say you won't tell him.' Her eyes filled with tears.

Suddenly, what had to me seemed a totally irrational response became totally rational. This young woman was petrified, quite understandably, and it was the underlying belief – the fear that she was going to lose her job – that was responsible for this violent outburst.

Although upset that I had unwittingly caused this person so much grief, at least taking the time at this stage to find out what was going on underneath the tip of the iceberg, gave me the opportunity to understand her behaviour and adjust my own accordingly, to achieve a positive outcome for both of us.

'Don't worry,' I reassured her, 'nobody need know. We'll read these questions through together.'

And that was what we did for the rest of the course, during which time I can happily report that the person who had been so aggressive for no *apparent* reason became my biggest fan.

MORAL

Remember the phrase:

Every behaviour has a positive intention

This is true even if the behaviour may not seem positive to you! It can be dangerous to take others' behaviour at face value. What you observe at the tip of the iceberg is very often hiding the fears and anxieties that are going on underneath. Our beliefs, values and sense of identity are the things that drive ours and others' behaviour.

REFLECTION

Influencing
Negotiation
Appreciating different people's maps of the world
Danger of making assumptions
Re-framing
Learning

17

INTRODUCTION

This classic fairy tale is one that most people can remember from their childhood, and I find that this short extract always proves to be a favourite with learning groups. It is interesting how it obviously takes on a different perspective with people when they see it in a context such as goal setting, rather than just a fairy tale.

THE TALE

Alice Meets the Cheshire Cat

'... The Cat only grinned when it saw Alice. It looked good-natured, she thought: still it had very long claws and a great many teeth, so she felt that it ought to be treated with respect.

'Cheshire Puss,' she began, rather timidly, as she did not at all know whether it would like the name: however, it only grinned a little wider. 'Come, it's pleased so far' thought Alice, and she went on.

'Would you tell me, please, which way I ought to go from here?'

'That depends a good deal on where you want to get to,' said the Cat.

'I don't much care where –' said Alice.

'Then it doesn't matter which way you go,' said the Cat.

' – so long as I get somewhere,' Alice added as an explanation.

'Oh, you're sure to do that,' said the Cat, 'if you only walk long enough.'

(Lewis Carroll, 1865)

MORAL

Those people without clear personal goals very often end up getting nowhere or helping to achieve other people's.

REFLECTION

Goal setting
Leadership and teambuilding
Motivation

18

INTRODUCTION

Some of the groups that I have been privileged to work with over the years have in some cases not received much in the way of what might be called formal education. And yet they very often have an inner wisdom and a wealth of natural knowledge lurking, sometimes in the depths of their minds. I think it is worth remembering, and saying – both to yourself and them – that each member of the group has survived very well without you so far!

THE TALE

Setting the World on Fire

I was working with a group of supervisors from a large printing company in the north of England. Most were in their mid 50s, all had worked with the company for many years, and in most cases had received little or no management training during that time.

The topic of the day was 'leadership and teambuilding', and I must admit we were struggling a bit with the concept, particularly as the group told me (almost proudly), that they believed they had never worked together as a team.

'What, *never*?' I asked, hoping to jog someone's memory.

They were adamant that such was the culture of the traditional company where they worked, that they had never experienced a feeling of team support or cohesion.

There followed a pregnant, almost defiant silence. Someone cleared his throat. Another folded his arms. My mind was frantically thinking up the next question. And then all of a sudden, Christine, who up until now had volunteered very little, said: '... except of course when we had "the fire" ...'

The rest of the group joined in, 'Ah, yes, but that was different, when we had the fire ...' the latter two words were spoken in almost reverent tones.

'Tell me about the fire,' I encouraged, attempting to sense the reverence of the occasion.

Christine went on to reminisce about this time, some ten years previous, when an extremely bad fire had almost wiped out the whole factory site.

'... but we all knew what we had to do,' she continued, almost in reverie, 'we had one goal, to get the place up and running as quickly as possible, everybody mucked in together, there was such a good atmosphere ...'

As she continued to talk, with the others chipping in their own personal memories, I walked to the flip chart and, unnoticed, started to write down the key words she mentioned:

One goal
Sense of direction
Synergy
Focus
Deadline
Team spirit
Humour
Enthusiasm
Positive thinking

When she'd finished, I pointed to the flip chart. It read like a chapter from a book on management theory. Christine's face reddened with pleasure and surprise.

'Did I say all that?' she asked, then added, as if by way of an apology, 'but I've never read any books on leadership.'

Books? Who said anything about books?

MORAL

This tale shows that the 'good stuff' in organizations – leadership and team work, motivation and empowerment – tends to turn up when we need it most, ie in a crisis. The challenge facing most organizations today is to find a way to unleash what is already there, without going round setting fire to things.

REFLECTION

Leadership and teambuilding
Motivation
Goal setting
Inspiration
Problem solving
Empowerment

19

INTRODUCTION

This retold classic Aesop fable is just as relevant today as it ever was. I have used this one as part of negotiation, influencing and assertiveness training seminars, to get across the point that aggression is not always the most effective way to win the day.

THE TALE

The Sun and the Wind

The Sun and the Wind once had an argument as to which of them was the stronger.

'I am the most powerful,' said the Sun.

'No, I am more powerful than you,' said the Wind.

While they were busy justifying their claims, they noticed a travelling man walking along a country road, his greatcoat buttoned up to his neck.

'Here's an opportunity to put our strength to the test,' said the Wind. 'Whoever can make that traveller take off his coat will be pronounced the stronger.'

The Sun agreed to the test.

First the Wind began to blow; he blew and howled and caused a great storm of rain and hail which got hold of the man's coat. But the more the Wind blew, the colder it became and the man simply fastened his coat more tightly around him. No matter what he did, the Wind could not get hold of that coat.

Then the Sun had his turn. He gently shone his rays around the man, warming his head, his shoulders and his back. And as it became warmer and warmer, the man first loosened his coat, then unfastened his coat and finally, looking up and smiling, he took off his coat to enjoy the warm day.

The Sun had won the prize!

MORAL

It is not always power, might and strength that wins the prize. Someone once told me that the ultimate power is powerlessness; the ultimate strength is gentleness. Think about it!

REFLECTION

Negotiation
Assertiveness
Influencing
Leadership and teambuilding

20

INTRODUCTION

I have used this poem as an inspirational and thought-provoking way to end seminars on personal development, assertiveness and self-esteem; its message seems to be one that most people can relate to some aspect of their lives. It encourages us to discover new ways of doing things and gives us the courage to do them.

THE TALE

Autobiography in Five Short Chapters

CHAPTER 1

I walk down the street
There is a deep hole in the sidewalk
I fall in
I am lost
It isn't my fault
It takes forever to find a way out.

CHAPTER 2

I walk down the same street
There is a deep hole in the sidewalk
I pretend I don't see it
I fall in again
I can't believe I'm in the same place
But it isn't my fault
It still takes a long time to get out.

CHAPTER 3

I walk down the same street
There is a deep hole in the sidewalk
I see it there
I still fall in

It's a habit
My eyes are open
I know where I am
It is my fault
I get out immediately.

CHAPTER 4

I walk down the same street
There is a deep hole in the sidewalk
I walk around it.

CHAPTER 5

I walk down another street.

Portia Nelson (1985)

MORAL

How many times do we become blinkered to thinking there is only one 'street' to walk down or one way of doing things? Taking a step back, and looking around, can give us a whole new perspective on our lives.

REFLECTION

Assertiveness
Goal setting
Re-framing
Problem solving
Self-esteem
Creativity

21

INTRODUCTION

David and Harvey used to run our local petrol station. Harvey was the serious, educated one, who played the organ at our local church (no comments, please) while David was the little, 'cheeky chappy, a joke and a smile for everyone' sort.

I tell this tale to dispel the myth that customer care is simply about smiling and chatting to all your customers. There are some situations when smiling and chatting can actually detract from making a sale.

THE TALE

'Did I Tell You the One About ...?'

Over a period of time, David had come to know and regard me as a 'regular'. I popped in for petrol once or sometimes twice a week, and I was clearly becoming a useful 'target' who could benefit from David's (exhaustive) philosophies of life. I suspect that everyone else in the village had long since become exhausted.

My trips to the petrol station – despite my protests to David and frequent tales of 'death and dishonour' if I were late – were taking longer and longer, and being too polite to say anything, I suffered in silence.

This particular day, I pulled up at the petrol station – in a hurry, as always. Hoping against hope that it would be the 'other one' on duty, I glanced in at the window while filling up the car. But no, this was not to be my lucky day. There was David, smiling, waving and waiting for me to go in to pay my dues and be subjected to his latest words of wisdom.

By now I had become accustomed to these little time-consuming forays – accustomed but not resigned. While filling up the car, I was musing on how I might finally get the message across to David that I was *in a hurry*! I decided that the best thing was to make it so obvious through word and deed that he would have to change his behaviour. Being somewhat theatrical, I thought, this should prove quite an easy task for me.

Having got my petrol, I flew into the shop, thinking myself into the role of 'Another Woman' – a combination between the French Lieutenant's woman and Mata Hari.

'Quick!' I gasped, holding a hand to my fevered brow, and using my best melodramatic voice, 'give me the bill; I'm drrrreadfully late ...'

David didn't flinch. 'Now you see,' he responded, slowly and thoughtfully, 'this is what I love about the Isle of Man.'

'Eh?' Mata Hari's veil had suddenly dropped.

'The Isle of Man,' replied David, by now in full nostalgic swing. 'You see no one's ever in a hurry there. They take things as they come. I can't wait for our holiday there. Did I tell you Harvey and I were going on holiday ...?'

I abandoned all hope of being on time for the meeting, listened stoically to the end of the story, paid my dues and left.

The next week I found another petrol station. The man behind the counter was old and grumpy but – best of all – silent.

MORAL

Treating others as you would like to be treated yourself might not always be appropriate!

REFLECTION

Customer care
Appreciating different people's maps of the world
Communication
Influencing

22

INTRODUCTION

A while ago, a close friend of mine was going through a bad time in her life. There seemed to be so many problems – work, health, relationships – and each one seemed to be linked in with all the others. Indeed, she described her life as 'a tangle'. I like to think this story was useful to her in helping her to separate the problems out again.

THE TALE

The Ball of Wool

I wanted to knit myself a jumper, a jumper with a sunflower on it, and when I asked for some wool, my mother directed me to the old cloth bag under the stairs.

The cloth bag was an old patchwork thing, with a gathered string for its neck, and it was into this that over the years, mother put all the remains from jumpers, scarves, cardigans and gloves that she had knitted for herself and the family.

When I went to open the bag – what a mess! All the individual bits of wool had tangled themselves together into one huge knot.

'It's hopeless!' I wailed to my mother. 'All the wool is tangled up together. I can't possibly knit a jumper with that. How could I even start to untangle it all?'

'It's easier than you think,' said mother. 'All you do is look for the easiest knot. When you undo that, the next knot will be easier too. And when you undo that, the next knot will be easier too. Just keep going, until all the wool is unravelled.'

I did as my mother told me to, and started to undo the first knot, and then the second knot and then the third. Sooner than I thought, the wool started to loosen and different colours began to emerge.

First I worked on the red wool. Then I worked on the yellow wool. Then I worked on the green wool. Then I worked on the grey wool. Very soon, instead of one huge knot, I had a number of neat balls of wool in front of me.

'You see,' said my mother, smiling, 'it's easier than you think. Now you can start to knit your jumper.'

As I started to knit, the pattern began to form. A sunflower, big and yellow and shining.

'Who would have thought,' I said to my mother, 'that such a beautiful sunflower was hiding in the old cloth bag of wool?'

'But it was there all the time,' my mother replied, 'it was just that you didn't know where to look.'

MORAL

I think the message of this tale is relevant to personal and work problems. One of the reasons why people become overwhelmed is when all the problems become knotted up together. It helps if we can begin to see each one as a separate issue and to work on one problem at a time.

REFLECTION

Problem solving
Motivation
Goal setting
Success not failure
Inspiration
Re-framing

23

INTRODUCTION

I use this true story as an illustration of the power of 'reverse psychology'. That is, if you know someone is always going to resist you, no matter what, you can turn that knowledge to your own advantage. But I always advise caution here: (a) because it can be seen as manipulative and (b) you have to be sure that the person concerned is going to resist. They might agree with you!

THE TALE

The Project

The group of supervisors I was working with were completing their first level of their supervisory management qualifications. As part of the programme, each member was required to research and complete a work-related project. Although this was a new and to some a daunting prospect, most of them tackled it valiantly.

But not Ralph. Ralph was in his late 50s, had never done anything like this before and clearly had no intention of starting now. And I could understand why. The main underlying problem was fear. And over the weeks that we had been meeting, I had done everything I thought possible to allay his (unspoken) fears and help him along. But every time I met with the same story from him, and the days had started to form their own monotonous pattern, which would go along these lines, 'So, Ralph, how's the project going?'

'I haven't done it. How can you expect me to do this project? My manager won't make time to see me, I don't have time away from production ...'

Over the weeks, the excuses became more creative, but the bottom line remained the same. *Ralph was not going to do his project.*

Towards the end of the course and the project deadline date, I realized that I had slipped into the same predictable 'doom loop' pattern as him, and neither of us was going anywhere. So working on the flexibility principle, the next week I tried a different approach.

'So, Ralph, how's the project going?'

'I haven't done it. How can you expect me to do this project? My manager won't make time to see me, I don't have time away from production ...'

'D'you know?' I said, thumping the table for impact, 'I've been thinking, and I think you're *absolutely right*.' There followed a stunned silence from Ralph. 'There is *no way* you can attempt this project. You don't have the time, your manager isn't helping you, you just can't do it. So, I've decided you shouldn't do it. Don't even attempt it. Whatever you do, Ralph, *do not do this project*!'

I walked away from the by now bewildered Ralph, wondering what on earth was going to happen next. As I got to the next table in the training room, I overheard him say to his colleagues, 'She's not going to tell *me* not to do my project ...'

The project was finished the next week. He passed with flying colours!

MORAL

If you always do what you've always done; you'll always get what you've always got.

If what you're doing isn't working – do something else!

REFLECTION

Re-framing
Success not failure
Problem solving
Appreciating different people's maps of the world
Influencing
Negotiation

24

INTRODUCTION

When I have been training people using unfamiliar concepts such as NLP or the creative uses of the brain, they sometimes become – understandably – rather bewildered, and a question I am very often asked by such groups is, 'But is all this true?' I don't know what is true, any more than anybody else does, but this wonderful story, beautifully written by John Fowles, helps me to answer the question.

THE TALE

The Prince and the Magician

Once upon a time there was a young prince who believed in all things but three. He did not believe in princesses, he did not believe in islands, he did not believe in God. His father, the king, told him such things did not exist. As there were no princesses or islands in his father's domains, and no sign of God, the young prince believed his father.

But then, one day, the prince ran away from his palace. He came to the next land. There, to his astonishment, from every coast he saw islands, and on these islands, strange and troubling creatures whom he dared not name. As he was searching for a boat, a man in full evening dress approached him along the shore.

'Are those real islands?' asked the young prince.

'Of course they are real islands,' said the man in evening dress.

'And those strange and troubling creatures?'

'They are all genuine and authentic princesses.'

'Then God also must exist!' cried the prince.

'I am God,' replied the man in full evening dress, with a bow.

The young prince returned home as quickly as he could.

'So you are back,' said his father, the king.

'I have seen islands, I have seen princesses, I have seen God,' said the prince reproachfully.

The king was unmoved.

'Neither real islands, nor real princesses, nor a real God, exist.'

'I saw them!'

'Tell me how God was dressed.'

'God was in full evening dress.'

'Were the sleeves of his coat rolled back?'

118

The prince remembered that they had been. The king smiled.

'That is the uniform of a magician. You have been deceived.'

At this, the prince returned to the next land, and went to the same shore, where once again he came upon the man in full evening dress.

'My father, the king, has told me who you are,' said the young prince indignantly. 'You deceived me last time, but not again. Now I know that those are not real islands and real princesses, because you are a magician.'

The man on the shore smiled.

'It is you who are deceived, my boy. In your father's kingdom there are many islands and many princesses. But you are under your father's spell, so you cannot see them.'

The prince returned pensively home. When he saw his father, he looked him in the eyes.

'Father, is it true that you are not a real king, but only a magician?'

The king smiled and rolled back his sleeves.

'Yes my son, I am only a magician.'

'Then the man on the shore was God.'

'The man on the shore was another magician.'

'I must know the real truth, the truth beyond magic.'

'There is no truth beyond magic,' said the king.

The prince was full of sadness. He said, 'I will kill myself.'

The king by magic caused death to appear. Death stood in the door and beckoned to the prince. The prince shuddered. He remembered the beautiful but unreal islands, and the unreal but beautiful princesses.

'Very well,' he said. 'I can bear it.'

'You see, my son,' said the king, 'you too now begin to be a magician.'

(From The Magus *by John Fowles, Jonathan Cape, 1977)*
© John Fowles, 1977. Kind permission for reproduction granted by Sheil Land
Associates.

MORAL

There is no such thing as reality and no such thing as magic – except in our own imaginations.

REFLECTION

Inspiration
Re-framing
Creativity
Learning

25

INTRODUCTION

My thanks go to the Storyteller's Association for introducing me to this tradi-
tional tale. Unfortunately, no one seems to be sure of its origins, so in true
storytelling tradition, I have retold it in my own words. Although it's a fairy tale,
I think that most people can relate to its powerful message, and it's a good way
of dealing with what are sometimes unspoken worries. I have used it as an
inspirational end to seminars on assertiveness, personal development and
self-esteem.

THE TALE

Giant Steps

Once upon a time, in a land far away, there lived an enormous giant. He
was at least ten feet tall, with a mop of red hair and a beard, and in his
hand he carried a mighty axe.

Every year, on the same day, at the same time, the giant would walk
down from the mountains which were his home, to stand outside the castle walls, terrorizing the inhabitants.

'Come, send me your bravest man, and I will fight him,' the giant would
shout, towering over the wall and waving his axe menacingly. 'Send me
someone to fight, or I will knock down your castle walls and kill everyone
with my axe.'

And every year, the gate in the castle wall would open slowly and fear-
fully, and one poor, valiant soul would walk out to face the foe and certain death.

'Is this the best you can do?' the giant would laugh mockingly. The
poor wretch would stand, mesmerized by the enormity of the giant and
the task in hand. Not one person had even managed to draw his sword,
before the giant would crush them with his mighty fist, and chop them
into tiny pieces with his axe.

But then one day, a young prince arrived in the town. 'Why does everyone here look so frightened and sad?' he asked a fellow traveller.

'You haven't seen the giant yet,' replied the traveller.

'What giant?' asked the young prince, intrigued.

The traveller told him the tale.

'Every year, on this very day, the giant arrives and challenges our bravest to a duel. And every year, he slays them exactly where they stand. They don't even move or draw their swords. It's as though the giant hypnotizes them.'

'We'll see about that,' said the young prince.

When the giant arrived later that day, he was waiting for him.

'Come, send me your bravest man, and I will fight him,' the giant shouted.

'I am here,' said the young prince, throwing open the gate, and striding out towards him.

For a moment, they stood and faced each other. Although he was still a long way away from him, the young prince was instantly struck by the sheer size and shocking appearance of his opponent.

But, summoning up all his courage, he started to walk towards the giant, brandishing his sword, and never taking his eyes off that dreadful face with the red hair and the red beard.

Suddenly, he realized that as he was walking, the giant – rather than appearing larger – actually began to shrink before his very eyes. He stopped and stared. The giant was only five feet tall.

He walked closer to him still then stopped and stared. Now the giant was only two feet tall. He continued walking until he was face to face with the giant, and each step he took, he saw the giant shrink. By now the giant was so small, that he looked up at the young prince. He was only 12 inches tall.

The young prince took his sword, and plunged it into the giant's heart.

As the giant lay dying on the ground, the young prince bent down and whispered to him, 'Who are you?'

With his dying breath, the giant replied, 'My name is Fear.'

MORAL

When you take action – the fear disappears!

REFLECTION

Success not failure
Assertiveness
Dealing with change
Empowerment
Inspiration
Self-esteem

26

INTRODUCTION

I was introduced to the work of poet, philosopher and artist, Kahlil Gibran, only a short time ago, but since then have been enchanted, like so many others, with the beauty of his work. The Prophet is a collection of poems, describing different aspects of life – love, joy and sorrow – and this one on teaching, which I thought particularly relevant for this book, and particularly inspirational for all those involved in learning and teaching of any kind.

THE TALE

The Prophet

Then said a teacher, Speak to us of Teaching.
And he said:

No man can reveal to you aught but that which already lies half asleep in the dawning of your knowledge.

The teacher who walks in the shadow of the temple, among his followers, gives not of his wisdom but rather of his faith and his lovingness.

If he is indeed wise he does not bid you enter the house of his wisdom, but rather leads you to the threshold of your own mind.

The astronomer may speak to you of his understanding of space, but he cannot give you his understanding.

The musician may sing to you of the rhythm which is in all space, but he cannot give you the ear which arrests the rhythm, nor the voice that echoes it.

And he who is versed in the science of numbers
can tell of the regions of weight and measure, but
he cannot conduct you thither.
For the vision of one man lends not its wings
to another man.

And even as each one of you stands alone in
God's knowledge, so must each one of you be
alone in his knowledge of God and in his understanding
of the earth.

(Kahlil Gibran, 1923)

From The Prophet *by Kahlil Gibran*
Copyright © 1923 by Kahlil Gibran and renewed 1951 by Administrators CTA of
Kahlil Gibran Estate and Mary G. Gibran.
Reprinted by permission of Alfred A. Knopf Inc.

MORAL

As teachers we should consider it a privilege to lead a person to the threshold of their own mind.

REFLECTION

Learning
Communication
Self-esteem
Inspiration

27

INTRODUCTION

This tale was told to me by a colleague who, in his student days, worked as a stage-hand at a local theatre. One year Larry Grayson, the British comedian, was on the bill, and he and my friend started to compare notes on the subjects of professionalism and tenacity. I have subsequently used the tale with professional sales people or others in the public eye to illustrate that anyone can do their job when they feel in the right mood to do it. The test comes when you don't feel like doing it!

THE TALE

The Professionals

In the early days, before he was a 'household name', Larry Grayson was working one season in a small provincial theatre in what might be called a less than receptive part of the country. This was the first night of the show.

Larry went on stage to do his one-man, stand up comedian act. It couldn't have been worse. The audience booed, shouted and threw assorted missiles at the stage, and when Larry came off, he went back to his dressing room, sat down and putting his head in his hands, he wept.

Time passed, and as he sat there still weeping, he heard a knock at the dressing-room door and a voice calling, 'Five minutes please, Mr Grayson. On stage in five minutes …'

Larry realized with horror that this was his call for the next matinée; he knew that he had to go back on the same stage, and go through the same torture – all over again.

Without stopping to think, Larry ceased his crying, dried his eyes, reapplied his make-up, and with his head held high, walked out of the dressing room in the direction of the stage …

MORAL

If at first you don't succeed, try, try, try again.

REFLECTION

Motivation
Success not failure
Inspiration
Self-esteem
Assertiveness

28

INTRODUCTION

This is a retold Aesop fable, which is great to use on assertiveness training, or if you're dealing with problem solving and decision making. I think it illustrates the point that although at times it is good to get advice, one can sometimes have too much of a good thing. Have courage in your own convictions!

THE TALE

The Miller, His Son and Their Donkey

A Miller, his son and their donkey were walking from one town to another, hoping to find someone to buy the donkey.

At the first hopeful town, they heard the people in the streets say:

'Would you believe it! Those two have a perfectly healthy animal, and they are both walking. What fools they are!'

The Miller heard them and thinking there might be some truth in what they said, hopped on the back of the donkey, while his son walked alongside.

At the next town they came to, the people said, 'Would you believe it! Look at that cruel Father, riding in luxury on the donkey, while his poor little son has to run to keep up. How selfish!'

The Miller heard them, and feeling ashamed of himself, he immediately got off the donkey and let his son ride instead.

They hadn't gone much further, when at the next town the people said, 'Would you believe it! Look how that lazy boy rides on the donkey, while his poor old father has to hobble along at the side. What a way to treat your elders!'

The Miller heard them and thinking there might be some truth in what they said, got on the donkey behind his son.

As the two of them rode on to the next town, a group of Travellers stopped them and one enquired, 'Is this donkey for sale?'

The Miller replied that it was.

'Would you believe it!' said the Traveller to his companions. This man is trying to sell his donkey. The poor thing will be exhausted, carrying such a heavy load. What a way to treat an animal!'

The Miller and his son not wanting to appear foolish, got off the donkey. The old man got some rope and a pole, and with his son's help, they tied the donkey to the pole, and carried him on their shoulders.

At the next town, the people came out to witness this ridiculous spectacle.

'Would you believe it! A man and his son carrying a donkey. What fools!'

They laughed and shouted and made fun of the Miller and his son.

Undeterred, the Miller and his son made their way through the town. However, as they were crossing the bridge, the ropes began to loosen and the donkey began to struggle. Halfway over the bridge, the donkey fell into the stream and was drowned.

MORAL

You can't please all of the people all of the time!

REFLECTION

Re-framing
Problem solving
Humour
Self-esteem
Assertiveness

29

INTRODUCTION

Some people in organizations place enormous and disproportionate faith in the power of committees, consultants, working parties, and strategy groups and the host of techniques, philosophies and other 'psycho-babble' that go along with them. The tendency is to focus on the symptoms without really knowing what the problem is! Having commissioned the report, or the training, or the conference, gives the instigator a sense of achievement and satisfaction – sometimes so much so that they don't feel inspired to do anything else with it.

THE TALE

Leave Well Alone

I was doing some work with a major organization in the public sector. I got into a conversation with the human resources manager one day, and she was recounting to me the type of 'teambuilding' events that they provided for their staff.

'We organize visits for them,' she said, 'and "away days", and trips to the bowling alley, and Outward Bound courses. It costs us a fortune!' But then she sighed, 'It doesn't seem to matter what we do, they don't seem to enjoy it.'

'What are you hoping to gain from doing it?' I asked, curious.

'Well, we want to encourage team working,' she replied, surprised I should ask such a naïve question.

'And does it?' I enquired.

'No!' she said. 'It doesn't make any difference at all.'

She sighed again.

'Funnily enough,' she continued, 'when we *don't* have any of these activities they work together really well ...'

Pondering on what she had just said for a moment, I cleared my throat and then ventured, 'Could I suggest something?'

'Yes please!' she said.

'Well, have you thought about – leaving them alone!'

'Aaaaah,' my colleague said, nodding sagely at my apparent words of wisdom.

I was tempted to send her an exorbitant bill for consultancy just to see if she paid it!

MORAL

If it ain't broke – why fix it?

REFLECTION

Dealing with change
Learning
Success not failure
Leadership and teambuilding
Danger of making assumptions
Empowerment

30

INTRODUCTION

This was a tale told by Milton Erickson, the well-known hypnotherapist, whose trance-inducing and therapeutic tales became known throughout the world for the benefit they brought to patients. This tale is good for illustrating the notion of 'going with the flow' and helping managers who are trying to guide their teams along the right road. Just keep reminding them of where the road is and let them do the rest!

THE TALE

The Horse on the Road

One day, when Erickson was a young man, a horse wandered into his family's yard. The horse had no identifying marks, and no one seemed to know who he belonged to. But, despite this, Erickson offered to try and return the horse to its owners.

He got on the horse, and rode it back to the road. He let the horse decide which way it wanted to go. From time to time, the horse wandered off the road or stopped to graze in a nearby field. Only on these occasions, did Erickson intervene by gently directing the horse back to the road.

Eventually, the horse arrived at the yard of a neighbour several miles down the road – and there it stopped.

The neighbour came out, and recognising his horse, thanked Erickson for returning him, and said, 'How did you know that was our horse and that he belonged here?'

Erickson replied, 'I didn't know – but the horse did. All I had to do was to keep him on the road.'

MORAL

Before you start worrying about how you're going to reach your destination, just make sure you know where your destination is!

REFLECTION

Goal setting
Success not failure
Leadership and teambuilding
Problem solving
Empowerment

31

INTRODUCTION

Occasionally, I feel some responsibility, and even a little sympathy – considering the hundreds of people that get to hear these stories – for the 'villain' of the piece. But then I console myself with the thought that all villains get what they deserve! This is a good tale to tell as part of communication or customer care training, to illustrate the danger of stereotyping people.

THE TALE

The Wedgwood China Shop

I don't know about you – but when I'm not at work, wearing my 'performance' outfit, I like to relax in what I call my 'scruffery' – jeans, T-shirt, that type of thing. And that's how I will tend to be seen, prowling the streets of Leeds or York, doing my shopping.

A long time ago, my husband and I bought a very expensive Wedgwood coffee set. God knows why! This is the sort of thing where each saucer costs the price of a three-piece suite, and to consider buying the coffee pot, you're talking in second mortgage terms. So, it's the sort of thing you accumulate over a period of time rather than buy outright.

Anyway, on this particular occasion, we had saved up our pennies, and thought we might be able to add – maybe a small sugar bowl – to the collection. In eager anticipation, we visited the local china shop.

We had only been there a statutory ten to fifteen seconds, when we were 'spotted' by one of the sales assistants – a reptilian type of man in his early 50s, tall and thin with greased black hair, and not a passing resemblance to Uriah Heap. My husband described him later as the sort of man who didn't have to open doors – he could slide underneath ...

'Can I help you?' he leered, bending over to greet us, rubbing his hands together and drooling.

'No thank you,' (the standard response) 'we have this particular coffee set, and are just looking to see what we might add to it.' (Translation: 'Go away and leave us alone, Uriah'.)

Now the chap slithers away to, oh, at least four feet away, and begins to 'dust things'. You've seen them do this. If it's not cleaning invisible

132

dust, then it's 'straightening things' that have already been straightened a thousand times before. And the really amazing thing is that these people have a built in skill. They can do all these chores without looking. Because all the time, their eyes are fixed on you and every micro-muscle movement.

No more than two minutes passed before he was back.

'If you know what piece you want ...' (drool) 'I'll check if we have it in stock.'

'No thank you,' (irritated voice) 'we're still just looking ...' (Translation: 'You're beginning to get to me, so butt out!')

This performance went on two or three times, Uriah exhausting himself with this rather ungainly 'dance' backwards and forwards.

In the end, I became so frustrated, I grabbed my husband by the arm and dragged him out of the shop.

'But I wanted a sugar bowl ...,' he bleated pathetically, as we were leaving the shop.

'Well,' I replied, 'we'll just to have to do without for another couple of years. Think of the money we've saved!'

MORAL

You can't always tell a book by its cover!

REFLECTION

Customer care
Communication
Danger of making assumptions
Humour

32

INTRODUCTION

The idea for this tale was given to me by a group of managers working in a manufacturing company in the Midlands. They had been asked to create their own metaphorical story to illustrate some difficult time in their department's history, and to suggest ways of how they might deal with it. I've expanded a little on their ideas. When asked to think of metaphors, people very often seem to come up with 'motion' ideas, like ships and sailing, climbing a rock face or striving to get somewhere.

THE TALE

The Pirate Ship

This was a ship that was going nowhere. Soon after setting sail, it had become apparent to the crew that their Captain had no sense of direction, no map, and very few navigational skills.

One day, mutiny broke out among them, and they cornered the Captain.

'Where are we going?' they bellowed at him.

'Well to tell the truth,' said the Captain, 'I have no idea. I left town in a bit of a hurry and forgot to pack the map ...'

As they were still arguing, they heard a loud commotion coming from their port side.

'Oh my God!' one of them cried, 'Pirates!'

Before they had time to think, let alone act, the pirates had boarded the ship, and were creating havoc, looting and pillaging all they could find. The sailors fought back as bravely as they could, but they were no match for the pirates, and there were quite a few casualties by the time the pirates – having taken all they could carry from the cargo – returned to their own ship.

'Now what, Captain?' said the First Mate, in a derisory voice. 'Where do we go from here?'

The Captain had just returned from a tour round the ship, to assess the damage.

'Well,' he said, 'one thing's for sure. That is never going to happen again – not to my ship. What we need is a plan ...'

Together, he and the First Mate, and some of the more senior sailors sat down in a group, and brainstormed some ideas. By the end of the day, they had come up with a mission statement for their voyage, a strategic plan and a rough map of the surrounding area.

'Right,' said the Captain, 'now we know where we're headed. Let's make sure that all the men know, and that they're willing to come along with us.'

The First Mate organized a team briefing session with all the sailors. He reported back to the Captain.

'They're happy with the plan, Cap'n,' he said, 'but some of them are unsure about the job they have to do.'

'Right,' said the Captain, 'we'll organize some training for them.'

And so all the sailors went through an intensive training programme, where they learnt the basics of navigation, swashbuckling, looting and pillaging.

'Now,' said the Captain, 'we're ready to set sail. And just wait till the next time we meet pirates ...'

MORAL

Every ship, however adventurous, needs some direction

REFLECTION

Motivation
Goal setting
Empowerment
Success not failure
Leadership and teambuilding

33

INTRODUCTION

This tale is one that was handed down to me, so I don't know its origins. I use it to illustrate the point that there is nothing new in teambuilding or leadership theories that hasn't already been thought of and exists in Nature. I have found that this tale works equally as well given out in written format, or spoken.

THE TALE

Lessons From The Geese

1. As each bird flaps its wings, it creates an uplift for the bird flying behind. Flying in a 'V' formation adds around 70 per cent greater flying range than if the bird was flying alone.

   Lesson: People who share a common direction can get where they are going quicker and more easily by getting a 'lift' from others in the team.

2. Whenever a goose falls out of formation, it suddenly feels the drag and resistance of trying to fly alone, and quickly gets back into formation to take advantage of the lifting power of the bird in front.

   Lesson: It is wiser to stay 'in formation' with those who are headed where we want to go, and be willing to accept their help as well as give ours to others in the team.

3. When the lead goose gets tired, it rotates back into formation and another goose takes the lead.

   Lesson: It benefits all in the team to take turns doing the hardest task and sharing the leadership.

4. The geese at the back of the 'V' honk to encourage those up in front to keep up their speed.

   Lesson: Only give your leader positive honking – no one likes a back-seat driver!

5. If a goose gets shot down or becomes sick two others drop out of formation and follow it down to help and protect it. They stay with it until it is either able to fly again or dies.

   Lesson: We too should stand by each other in the difficult times as well as the prosperous ones.

MORAL

There is a lot to be learned from Nature which can be applied to our own lives.

REFLECTION

Leadership and teambuilding
Motivation
Inspiration
Problem solving

34

INTRODUCTION

This true tale has a sad but cautionary message; we shouldn't allow ourselves to become so overwhelmed by rules and regulations as to ignore the basic common sense of management or its human aspects. It is a useful tale to tell in any situation where you are encouraging people to think more creatively, rather than simply sticking blindly to the rules.

THE TALE

The 'Correct' Procedure

This tale goes back about ten years ago; the large retailer with whom I was working at the time was going through the same difficult stage as so many, that is, making the transition from being a family firm to being an enormous, nationwide operation.

Someone decided that what was needed to help the process along was a set of rules and regulations. And someone slaved for many hours to produce a procedures manual, a huge, weighty tome, which was designed to describe every incident known to man and how to deal with them.

The manual was not greeted by the same enthusiasm with which it had been produced. People said they felt stifled, that it stunted their creativity, and took away any feelings of empowerment that they might have.

During the course of one particularly 'heavy' management meeting I remember a heated discussion ensuing between the general manager and the catering manager. The general manager said,

'Look, with such large numbers of people, we need standardization and consistency. This manual tells you what to do in any possible situation. We can't afford for people to be doing things their own way.'

'I can appreciate that,' the catering manager replied, 'but what happens to flexibility, or our authority as managers to do what we think is best? What happens to our creativity, the human touch ...'

He was interrupted by a knock at the door. The door opened and one of the catering assistants appeared.

'I'm sorry to interrupt,' she said, breathlessly and obviously upset, 'but the cook has just attempted suicide. What shall we do?'

The catering manager, without picking up his procedures manual, silently left the room.

MORAL

Procedures are there to serve – not to be served

REFLECTION

Empowerment
Creativity
Problem solving
Dealing with change

35

INTRODUCTION

We travel miles, and are prepared to pay a fortune, to meet with people who can inspire and educate us – not realizing that sometimes they are actually sitting on our doorstep. I use this tale as part of seminars on self-esteem and assertiveness and also to encourage people to see the positive rather than the negative incidents in life.

THE TALE

John's Tale

You probably won't have heard of John Foxley. He wasn't a famous politician or a movie star or someone in the City. He didn't win any prizes or awards or gold medals in the Olympics.

John worked as a sales representative for a shipping company in the north of England. He was one of those rare breed of people, decent, honest and industrious, a man of high integrity and devoted to his wife Susanne and their two young children.

John's career had not been an easy one. He had been made redundant so many times that he and his wife began to view it as a way of life. But he was always philosophical about it – something would turn up – and if he felt any bitterness, he never ever showed it.

Shortly before the Christmas of 1995, just when he was feeling settled and doing well in his job, the company suffered a financial set-back – and John was made redundant again. He and Susanne looked forward apprehensively to the Christmas that was to come, and wondered what they would be able to afford in the way of presents for the two children.

When he lost the job, he also lost the car. But, not deterred, John would walk or bicycle the five miles into the nearest town to visit the Jobcentre and recruitment agencies. He became a familiar – and always cheerful – sight around the village.

'Carry your bags, Lady?' he joked with me one day, when he saw me struggling home with some shopping.

We stopped and chatted. He was confident, as always, that another job was just around the corner.

The next time I heard of John Foxley, only a week later, it was the news that he had died of a heart attack. He was just 49.

When I went to commiserate with Susanne, his widow, she told me that just two days before he died, John had indeed found a new job, which he had been looking forward to starting in the new year. I was struck with what seemed to me to be the awful irony of the circumstances. But Susanne smiled and said, 'Please don't think of it as tragic – because I know that John wouldn't. He was thrilled that he had found another job. He was looking forward to the future. And he always said he never wanted to be 50! His life was a triumph, not a tragedy.'

MORAL

Life can be either a triumph or a tragedy and that doesn't depend just on the circumstances that present themselves, but also on how we view them.

REFLECTION

Inspiration
Re-framing
Success not failure
Self-esteem

36

INTRODUCTION

I'm very often alarmed by the obvious fear with which some people contemplate the idea of learning or training. Although the woman in this tale was an extreme case, there are many others – normal, sane, mature individuals like you and me – who are frightened to death of what is in store for them. I think it's our responsibility, as trainers or managers, to do all we can to allay their fears.

THE TALE

Role Play

I was preparing the training room for a course which I was running for the local council. I felt a tap on my shoulder.

'Excuse me,' the man said, 'do you think I could have a word with you about one of my staff who is coming on your course today?'

'Of course,' I said, waiting for him to explain.

'Not here ...' he said secretively, beckoning to the corridor outside.

Intrigued, I followed him out of the training room. In the corridor stood a young woman, in her mid-twenties. Her face had a pallor that shocked me; her hand looked like it was welded onto the door handle and she was almost shaking with fear.

'This is Ann,' her manager explained, 'she hates training.'

Well, that was an interesting introduction I thought.

'Hello, Ann,' I said, 'what do you hate about training?'

'She particularly hates doing role plays,' answered her manager on her behalf, while Ann nodded mutely.

'Do you?' I gasped in mock disbelief. 'So do I! Thank God we're not doing them today!'

Ann started to smile – just a little bit – but her hand remained fixed on the door handle.

'But there's another thing,' said her manager, 'you see, Mick is going to be on the same course today, and he can be well, vocal. Ann is a bit frightened of him.'

'Is he a bit difficult, this Mick?' I asked Ann. She nodded.

'He's not going to give me a hard time is he?' She smiled again.

'He might' she ventured.

'Oh God,' I continued, 'I hate people like that. Do you think you could help me deal with him? I mean, you know him better than I do. I could do with you there for protection. What do you say?'

'I'll stay till lunch time,' said Ann.

'Fine,' I said, 'I should have got the measure of him by then.' We walked hand in hand back into the training room.

During the course of the day, Ann was quiet – but she took a full part in the proceedings – and after lunch, much to my surprise, she returned for the afternoon session.

At periodic intervals during the day, I went up to her and whispered, 'How do you think I'm doing?'

'OK' she grinned.

I met Ann again some months later in a follow-up course. She had matured and blossomed considerably, and I was pleasantly surprised when she volunteered to be the spokesperson for her group in one of the exercises.

I often wonder if she really thinks I have a fear of role plays and of people called Mick. Maybe I have or maybe that's just another role play.

MORAL

I can't think of a better message than Wordsworth's immortal lines:

Pleasure and learning go hand in hand, but pleasure leads the way

REFLECTION

Appreciating different people's maps of the world
Re-framing
Success not failure
Learning
Assertiveness

37

INTRODUCTION

This is a retold Sufi teaching tale whose origins are said to date back to the ninth century. It is one of those tales with a certain air of mystery, which I have found is most effective to tell at the end of a day, particularly if you have been dealing with such issues as dealing with change or creativity.

THE TALE

How the Waters Changed

One day, many thousands of years ago, the whole of mankind was given a warning. Khdir, who was Moses' teacher, summoned all the people together saying, 'I give you warning, that very soon, all the water in the world is going to dry up. And when it does, it will eventually be replaced with new water, which will make anyone who drinks it insane. You must make provision now and store away as much of the pure water as you can.'

Only one man out of the thousands there listened and understood Khdir's message. He toiled night and day making journeys from the river to his cave, storing as much of the pure water as he could.

On the date that Khdir had predicted, sure enough, all the rivers and streams dried up, and all the wells ran dry and the man who had listened to Khdir's message did as he was instructed, and went back to his hide-out and drank his preserved water.

And after a short time, as Khdir had also predicted, the water began to flow again but the water was unpure and made all who drank it insane. Out of curiosity the man who had his own reserve of water went to meet with some of the people who had been his friends. But he found that the men who drank this new water were talking and acting in very strange ways, and they had no recollection of him or of Khdir's warning.

He realized with horror, as he tried to talk to them and reason with them, that they thought *he* was the madman – and some of them were hostile towards him, and some of them were compassionate – but none of them was understanding.

So, for some time, the lone man returned to his cave each day to drink his carefully preserved water. But in the end, he could bear the loneliness and isolation no longer. He drank the new water, and became mad just like the rest.

In years to come, he became known as the man who had been mad and miraculously restored to sanity.

MORAL

It takes courage to be the one who listens, learns and understands, and the one who stands their ground. Sometimes it is easier to give up and go with the flow of the rest.

REFLECTION

Re-framing
Creativity
Dealing with change
Inspiration
Learning

38

INTRODUCTION

I have worked for a number of years with the British Printing Industries Federation, and through them run a range of workshops for managers and supervisors within the industry. It always intrigues me to think that these groups believe they are learning from me when I'm sure the reverse is far more often the case! I have used this tale on presentation skills seminars, which it seems most managers seem to dread, to put the topic into a different context.

THE TALE

Rodney's Tale

Rodney was a supervisor from a large printing company in Leeds, and formed part of the group going through their first supervisory training. He was in his mid-30s, intelligent, personable, highly thought of in his job and completely deaf.

Neither he, nor his company – nor me – were sure that we could cope with the course, but we all agreed to give it a go. Rodney came with an interpreter who would 'sign' whatever I or other members of the group were saying, and after a few weeks we all settled into an effective and rather enjoyable routine.

I immediately learnt that I had picked up some very bad habits over the years that I had been involved in training – like turning to the flip chart and carrying on talking, talking with my hand over my mouth, or just mumbling unintelligibly. Having Rodney there was a great education for me.

The courses themselves are always enjoyable for both me and the participants. One thing I had to get used to was the fact that after something humorous had been said, two seconds later, there would be a burst of laughter from Rodney. It was like speaking over a transatlantic phone, with a time delay.

'Come on Rodney,' I used to say, laughing, 'these are the jokes ... keep up.'

On the day that we dealt with communication skills, I was somewhat perturbed as to how Rodney would cope with the group presentation that was an integral part of the course. I needn't have worried. In fact,

146

when the group split into two for their presentations, I was actually more concerned with the other group, who were having the customary histrionics. Nobody seems to like learning presentation skills.

'Well, if I have to do a presentation, that's *it*,' said one chap, 'I can't do it ... petrified ...'

The first group stood up to do their presentation, and to most people's surprise, Rodney was one of the first to speak. Although he wasn't profoundly deaf, you could still tell when you heard his voice that he had severe hearing difficulties. And nobody doubted that this exercise was a difficult thing for him to do but he did it, with courage and dignity.

When he had finished, I turned and looked at the other group. No further comment was necessary. Somewhat ashamedly, they all stood up to take their turn.

MORAL

The bravery of some people is an inspiration to us all.

REFLECTION

Inspiration
Success not failure
Learning
Re-framing

39

INTRODUCTION

I sometimes feel sympathy for groups of managers at the end of a period of train-ing when they are left to get back to the 'real world' and carry out all the won-derful theories and notions that we have discussed. I use this 'prayer' as an end to training, particularly where leadership has been covered. I think it is a good, if slightly irreverent way to lighten the proceedings. In terms of delivery, if you're going to read this one out aloud, take some time to practise, as there are some quite tricky pronunciations.

THE TALE

A Leader's Prayer

Dear Lord,

Help me to become the kind of leader my management would like to have me be. Give me the mysterious something which will enable me at all times satisfactorily to explain policies, rules, regulations and procedures to my workers even when they have never been explained to me.

Help me to teach and to train the uninterested and dim-witted without ever losing my patience or my temper.

Give me that love for my fellow men which passeth all understanding so that I may lead the recalcitrant, obstinate no-good worker into the paths of righteousness by my own example, and by soft persuading remon-strance, instead of busting him on the nose.

Instil into my inner-being tranquillity and peace of mind that no longer will I wake from my restless sleep in the middle of the night crying out

'What has the boss got that I haven't got and how did he get it?'

Teach me to smile even if it kills me.

Make me a better leader of men by helping develop larger and greater qualities of understanding, tolerance, sympathy, wisdom, perspective, equanimity, mind-reading and second-sight.

And when, Dear Lord, Thou has helped me to achieve the high pinnacle my management has prescribed for me, and when I shall have become the paragon of all supervisory virtues in this earthly world, Dear Lord, move over.

'A Leader's Prayer' from Understanding Organizations *by Charles B. Handy*
(Penguin Books 1976), Third edition 1985).
Copyright © Charles B. Handy, 1976, 1981, 1985.

MORAL

We're all human after all!

REFLECTION

Leadership and teambuilding
Inspiration
Humour
Re-framing

40

INTRODUCTION

Sitting as I do in my office, surrounded by inspirational books on empowerment, democratic leadership and the like, it is easy to lose sight of the fact that, sadly, there is sometimes a huge gap between theory and reality. I find when I've told this true story to people they are – quite rightly – shocked to think that such a lack of understanding still exists in some organizations, and apparently at senior levels. But, although it's difficult to understand, it is reality nevertheless. Let's hope that it's changing.

THE TALE

'Just a Bod'

I remember working with a small manufacturing firm who were thinking about introducing a performance appraisal system. It was something they had never contemplated before, and they wanted to know the 'right' way to go about it. The first stage of the process was a meeting between myself and the senior management team. Having talked about the reasons for doing it, the benefits to be gained and so on, we started to consider the practicalities, such as timing and administration.

'Well, we haven't decided who we're going to appraise yet,' said the managing director.

'Aren't you going to appraise everyone?' I asked, somewhat surprised, as I didn't even consider it as an option.

'Good God, no!' said the finance director. 'We're only going to appraise managers, supervisors and administration staff. We're not going to bother with the production lot!'

My jaw dropped as he carried on, 'Well, I mean how would you do it? It's just a 'bod' after all isn't it, sitting at the end of a machine. How could you possibly appraise him?'

All eyes turned to me. Resisting the strong urge to throttle the finance director, I calmed myself by asking him instead, 'I wonder ... do you suppose these 'bods' have feelings?'

A silence fell on the proceedings. Eventually, the managing director, picking up the tension of the situation said, 'What would you do?'

I gave the impartial consultant's answer and told them that, at the end of the day, it was their decision, but that I could give them a pretty sure guarantee that if they started to discriminate in terms of who did and didn't get an appraisal interview, they would land themselves in deep water.

When they eventually started the procedure, some weeks later, I was relieved to discover that *all* their staff were being appraised – even the bods.

MORAL

It is a common mistake still made in business to assume that, because people are doing mundane jobs, they have mundane minds and this is not the case. It is also very dangerous to make decisions about these people based on the content of the job that they do.

REFLECTION

Appreciating different people's maps of the world
Danger of making assumptions
Leadership and teambuilding
Appraisal

41

INTRODUCTION

Most people, unless they are keen fitness fiends, can relate to this pathetic little tale! It is useful in illustrating the notion of self-image, and how that might compare with how others see us. Although I can laugh about it now, at the time the experience was quite devastating until I saw it from a different point of view, and realized how singularly unimportant it was in the greater scheme of things. But it's amazing what power other people can hold over us.

THE TALE

Fitness for the Purpose

I do try to exercise regularly – well, at least twice a year – but when my friendly local club folded recently, I made the fatal mistake of joining a large, established aerobics class in the city. I don't know if you've ever joined a class like this, one that's made up of about 20 people who have apparently been coming to the same class for at least half a lifetime and know *all* the right steps. Well, let me tell you, it's not the most motivating of experiences particularly if like me your main objective in going was to make yourself feel better and improve your self-esteem.

The first blow to the ego comes when you discover that your well-worn shorts and T-shirt, which were quite acceptable at the village community centre, are now somewhat inadequate in comparison with the designer lycra outfits that surround you on every side.

The second blow comes when you actually get into the exercises, which are accompanied by obligatory ear-splitting music, and a screaming instructor who at periodic intervals insists on yelling at the assembled group, 'And ... *turn!*'

The result of this repeated command is that the 20 bodies all uniformly and elegantly rotate to face in the opposite direction, which unfortunately just happens to be looking directly at you, as you are the only one who has turned the wrong way.

I suffered an hour of these, and yet more humiliating experiences, and when finally released, ran – or rather limped – back to my car, vowing never to venture out in public again. How could I have been so stupid as to think I could join in with these demi-gods? Why did my body not work in the same co-ordinated and gazelle-like way that theirs did? Why was I such a failure in the fitness fanatics league?

The following week, still pondering on these questions, but having scraped together at least some of my shattered ego, I happened to be running a training course at the same hotel where my ill-fated aerobics class was based.

The day had been very successful, the group had enjoyed the training, and had all come up to me afterwards to say goodbye, shake hands and thank me for my efforts. I was quietly congratulating myself on a job well done.

As I loaded my car, I looked across nervously at the gymnasium, the scene of my torment and humiliation so little time ago. The gym is housed in a sort of conservatory, and the windows are all double-glazed, so watching the scene from the outside was a bit like watching television with the sound turned down.

I was amazed with the sight that greeted me. Some 20 heavy sweating bodies were there, all pulling ridiculous contortions, with matching facial expressions. I didn't see any elegance; there was no hint of poetry in motion. Even the designer lycra had lost it appeal.

I stopped in my tracks, and watched them quite openly.

Could these be the same demi-gods who had made me feel such a lesser mortal only a week ago? Surely these weren't the same superhumans that had caused me so much pain and humiliation?

As I stood there looking in, I suddenly caught sight of a reflection in the glass; it was a tall, slim, quite elegantly dressed woman, who looked calm and confident and rather self-assured. I realized it was me ... and I started to laugh.

MORAL

Every person excels at something; the important thing to remember is that we don't all excel at the same thing. The temptation is to compare our worst with somebody else's best and it's not a healthy comparison. Remember the phrase – even a stopped clock is right twice a day! Shortly after this experience, I saw a card in a gift shop that I just had to buy. It says:

Aerobics: Just my little way of paying money to humiliate myself in public

REFLECTION

Re-framing
Self-esteem
Success not failure
Assertiveness
Humour

42

INTRODUCTION

I'm amazed the number of times I meet a production worker who has no idea where the company's sales department is. Or an administrative assistant who has no idea what happens in the accounts department. Although this is a 'family' tale, it might not be as unrelated as you think to modern business life.

THE TALE

All Those Buns!

My husband's grandmother was well into her 80s when she died a few years ago. In all that time, she had only once ventured outside her home of Carlton, which is a tiny village on the outskirts of Barnsley, in South Yorkshire. She had never learnt to drive; she had never flown in an aeroplane. She lived in a different generation.

When the Lyon's cake company elected to build their new, enormous factory a couple of miles down the road from her home, grandmother was puzzled.

'Why on earth have they built that great big thing here?' she said one day, while being driven past the new building, and then added with an authoritative air, 'They'll never sell all those buns in Carlton!'

MORAL

We all have times when we can't see further than our own noses.

REFLECTION

Re-framing
Creativity
Dealing with change
Empowerment
Humour

43

INTRODUCTION

A book of tales would not be complete without a contribution from one of the world's best known storytellers – Rudyard Kipling. I think most people are familiar with the opening lines of this well-known poem. They are very often used to illustrate the importance of open-ended questions in sales or communications training. However, the latter part of the poem is less well-known, but I think it's still relevant for the same type of topics.

THE TALE

Six Honest Serving-Men

I keep six honest serving-men
(They taught me all I knew)
Their names are What and Why and When
And How and Where and Who.
I send them over land and sea
I send them east and west;
But after they have worked for me,
I give them all a rest.

I let them rest from nine till five,
For I am busy then,
As well as breakfast, lunch, and tea,
For they are hungry men:
But different folk have different views:
I know a person small –
She keeps ten million serving-men,
Who get no rest at all!
She sends 'em abroad on her own affairs,
From the second she opens her eyes –
One million Hows, two million Wheres,
And seven million Whys!

Rudyard Kipling, 'The Elephant's Child' (1902)
Reproduced with kind permission of A P Watt Ltd on behalf of the National Trust

MORAL

There are times when we need to stop the questioning and start listening to the answers!

REFLECTION

Communication
Problem solving
Customer care
Learning

44

INTRODUCTION

Reports vary as to whether or not this is actually a true tale. However, it is a powerful illustration of the effect that our beliefs can have on our behaviour and even if it wasn't true of Houdini, it could be true for any one of us! I have used this tale on seminars where I am encouraging people to identify, and start to change, their own limiting beliefs.

THE TALE

Houdini and the Locked Door

Harry Houdini, the famous American escapologist, had become so accomplished in his art, that he started to issue challenges to people to find him the strongest box, or cage or water barrel, and the most secure or complex system of chains and locks, so that he could show off his prowess.

A bank in England had made a safe that they claimed was impenetrable, and they contacted Houdini to dare him to try and break out of it.

Houdini could not resist the challenge. He went to England to prove the safe-makers wrong.

After he was bound and locked in the safe, Houdini went through his normal routine. He had developed the process to such a fine art over the years that he was supremely calm and confident that he could pick the lock of the door.

But after the first hour, Houdini was not feeling quite so calm. He had used up all his normal manoeuvres without success. With sweat now pouring off him, he began to struggle and pull at the lock. But no matter what he tried, the lock would not budge.

After two hours, Houdini was totally exhausted. He fell against the huge door of the safe ... which moved and swung open. The door had never been locked in the first place!

But in Houdini's mind that door was more secure than it ever could have been if it had been locked.

MORAL

Henry Ford said:

If you think you can, or you think you cannot – you're absolutely right!

If something is true for us then it's true, no matter what other people might tell us. If you want to change your behaviour, start first with changing your beliefs.

REFLECTION

Motivation
Re-framing
Goal setting
Self-esteem

45

INTRODUCTION

I use this true story when I'm encouraging groups to be creative and use their 'right brains', and to illustrate the dangers of restricted thinking. And I know what you'll say when you've read it – '... and just think, she could have been a millionaire by now.' I know – you don't have to remind me!

THE TALE

Revolution In Your Mind

When I worked as personnel manager for a large supermarket chain years ago, we used to have the perennial problem of what to do with the checkout operator who sat directly in front of the main entrance.

In summer, when it was hot, or as hot as it gets in England, the sun used to stream in right through the glass doors directly onto the back of the operator.

But probably more of a problem came in the winter when the doors would be constantly opening and closing with the hundreds of customers that came through in a day, and the cold draughts were unbearable.

At the weekly meetings between management and staff, when you could be sure that the subject would always arise, we racked our brains for a solution. All we had come up with so far was either to rotate the schedules of the operators, so they all had an equal share of torture – or, even more inventive, to let them wear a body-warmer type of waistcoat in the winter which would go some way (but only a little way) to keeping off the cold.

On this particular occasion, the problem arose again.

'Well, we can't go on like this,' said the supervisor in charge. 'Some of the operators are saying it's making them ill, being in the cold all the time. We'll have to think of something.'

'Well, we've tried various things,' I said, 'and nothing seems to work. Has anybody else any bright ideas?'

A long silence descended on the meeting. Eventually one woman, a checkout operator, who had worked for us for a long time, piped up,

'Instead of the conventional doors we have now that just open and close one way, why don't we have a revolving door that would stop the draft getting in?'

Her idea was greeted with hilarity from the group – and me.

'Well, that's a daft idea, Gladys.' I said, 'How on earth do you think we would get trolleys through a revolving door?'

There was more hilarity from the group, and Gladys, looking embarrassed, kept quiet. In the absence of any more creative ideas, we resolved to go on wearing the body-warmers ...

Nowadays, every time I go through one of the outsized, trolley-sized, revolving doors that are present in virtually every supermarket in England I blush, and think of Gladys. I wonder if she's made her first million yet?

MORAL

Beware of the negative effects of restrictive, 'left-brain' thinking. When the term 'revolving door' was mentioned, I immediately conjured up in my mind the things that I'd seen in hotels that are normally just one person's width. But who was to say you couldn't have a huge revolving door, big enough for a trolley and a person to get through?

REFLECTION

Creativity
Re-framing
Empowerment
Dealing with change

46

INTRODUCTION

I wrote this tale when I was taking my practitioner training in NLP. We were asked to pair up with another person, and write a metaphorical type story that might help our partner with a particular issue. My partner had been having some problems in the company she was working with. The culture was very 'get-up-and-go' and people were expected to look busy and dynamic, and dash around all day. But my partner's natural style tended more towards the methodical, 'reflector' approach. Although she was extremely successful in her role, she found herself on the horns of a dilemma …

THE TALE

The Tortoise and the Hare Revisited

Once upon a time, there was a Tortoise called Cecil, and a Hare called Horace, and they both lived on Farmer Smith's land.

Every day, they would both go down to the pond to drink. Cecil would be ready at 8 o'clock in the morning, and he would plod along slowly and steadily until he reached the pond. There he would have a long, slow, enjoyable drink of the cool water. It made him feel refreshed and alive and full of energy. He was ready to start his day.

Horace, on the other hand, usually slept in, and wouldn't set off for the pond until 9 o'clock. At some point every day, he would scream past Cecil, usually knocking him sideways and he would always reach the pond first. When he reached the pond, Horace would gulp down the water so fast that it made him feel ill and bloated and he would have to rest on the bank for at least half an hour before getting his breath back.

One day, while Horace was lying on the bank wondering to himself why he went through this performance every day, Cecil arrived to drink at the pond.

Horace, trying not to sound breathless said, 'Don't you get tired of being so slow? Your life is *so* boring compared to mine. Wouldn't you like to be fast and dynamic like me, and have people notice you and admire you?'

162

Cecil thought for a minute and said, 'It's true, you always get to the pond before me, and you're fast and dynamic and I know that people are impressed with your style.

'However, I am quite happy with my life, because I keep a cool head when I walk and I can take in the scenery, and enjoy the quality of the flowers and the trees and the birds.

'I also have time to think as I walk and I plan the best and most effective route to take to the pond. And when I have taken the best route, I reach the pond still with plenty of energy left to enjoy my drink. And I always have plenty of strength to walk back and enjoy the odd lettuce leaf on the way.'

As Horace tried to think of something witty to say, but realized he didn't have the energy, Cecil continued, 'And you know, Horace, people who know both of us say that they do admire you because of your speed and your dynamism, and your 'get-up-and-go'.

'But they also admire me, although for different reasons. They see me as being someone they can rely on; I am careful and I plan ahead, and I always give myself time to think of the most effective way of doing things. And because I think ahead, I always have energy to do whatever jobs I need to do.

'And at the end of it all Horace, it *is* a big pond. And we *do* both get to drink the water.'

MORAL

Even though there's only one winner, both the Tortoise and the Hare do complete the race.

REFLECTION

Success not failure
Re-framing
Self-esteem
Assertiveness
Appreciating different people's maps of the world

47

INTRODUCTION

I don't very often tell this tale to groups, as I can't do it without bawling my eyes out, but I do think it serves as a salutary reminder of how fortunes can be so easily reversed, and how we need to get our own lives into perspective from time to time.

THE TALE

'Thank You for the Smile'

I always find it heartbreaking to see the increasingly common sight of beggars on the street in my local city. Whatever you think about the politics of the situation or the circumstances that brought them there in the first place, it is still none the less a situation that reminds us – it could just as easily have been me sitting there, or you.

The sight is even more poignant when you realize how young some of these beggars are, and ironical that they are begging for money in the middle of what is thought by most to be an affluent city.

One day, while walking through the city, with a thousand important and pressing things on my mind, I was annoyed when I nearly fell over a bundle of dirty clothes in a shop doorway. To my horror, I realized when the bundle of clothes moved, that it was in fact a young person, a boy, probably no more than 14 or 15. He stretched out his hand to me, and for an awful moment the scene was reminiscent of Jesus meeting the leper colony.

'Could you spare some loose change?' the voice was faint, and hopeless.

Like most people in these situations, with emotions ranging somewhere between guilt, embarrassment and despair, I hastily dug in my pocket for some change which I gave to the boy, and hurried past.

'Excuse me,' the voice called out after me. I turned back, surprised, wondering what further request my already guilt-ridden mind was going to be subjected to.

'Thank you for the smile,' the boy said, 'I don't usually get that.'

I nodded and then turned away. I had intended to say 'You're welcome' or 'Don't mention it' – but I found I couldn't speak.

MORAL

There, but for the grace of God, go you and I.

REFLECTION

Inspiration
Re-framing
Appreciating different people's maps of the world
Danger of making assumptions

48

INTRODUCTION

The parables of Jesus have been told for thousands of years, to young and old alike. What makes them so effective and so memorable is their simplicity and the fact that – whatever age we live in – their messages are timeless. This particular parable is one that most people can remember from their childhood, and I use it when covering areas such as learning, teaching or even change management .

THE TALE

The Parable of the Sower and the Seed

A Sower went forth to sow; and when he sowed, some of the seed fell by the wayside, and the birds came and devoured them up; some fell upon stony ground, where there was not much earth. They sprang up, but when the sun shone, they were scorched, and because they had no root, they withered away. Some fell among thorns, and the thorns sprang up and choked them.

But others fell into good ground, and brought forth fruit, some a hundredfold, some sixtyfold and some thirtyfold.

The disciples said to Jesus, 'Why do you talk to us in parables? What does this mean?'

And Jesus said, 'The seed is the word of God. Those by the wayside are they that hear; then comes the devil and takes away the word out of their hearts, lest they should believe and be saved.

'They on the rock are they which, when they hear, receive the word with joy; but there is no foundation to their belief, and in the time of temptation, it falls away.

'And that which fell among thorns are they which, when they have heard, go forth and are choked with cares and riches and pleasures of this life, and bring no fruit to perfection.

'But that on the good ground are they which, in an honest and good heart, having heard the word, keep it, and bring forth fruit with patience.'

MORAL

In the ancient book of Parables that I was reading, an unknown author had written this moral: 'We know the sower, all of us. We meet him every day. He sows the truth in many a field, in books and pulpits and papers, in schools and marketplaces. And some listen and forget, some listen and care nothing; some listen and believe, and those who believe are the saviours of the world.'

REFLECTION

Learning
Inspiration
Dealing with change

49

INTRODUCTION

I have made mention in another of the tales that although I have studied neuro-linguistic programming for a number of years I still find it difficult to think of an easy definition. This story is an account of my first – and probably last – attempt.

THE TALE

Say What You Mean and Mean What You Say

I hadn't been self-employed for very long, but I had made enough money to book myself on a practitioner course in London, to study neuro-linguistic programming.

I was staying in the hotel where the course was being held. The first morning, eager and excited at the start of a new adventure, I went down to the dining room for breakfast.

It was very busy in the dining room, and I found myself sharing a small table with an elderly, white-haired, old-colonial sort of gentleman. After the opening pleasantries, we got into a more in-depth conversation.

'What are you here for?' he asked.

'I'm doing a training course,' I answered proudly.

'Oh, that's interesting,' said the old man, 'What's it on?'

'Neuro-linguistic programming,' I answered, with even more of a swagger. I was keen to demonstrate that I had at least reached the stage where I could pronounce the name without hesitation – well, just about.

But the old man's next question quickly took away any of the mis-placed confidence that I might have been feeling.

'Oh ... and what's that exactly?'

I felt the panic rise in my chest. Yes, what was it? How could I begin to describe it? I looked heavenward in the hope of some divine intervention. I thought of all the 'clever' things I had read by experts on the topic, like Bandler and Grinder and Dilts. What would they have said? Perhaps I should reply to his question in the form of some clever, but completely incomprehensible metaphor, which would leave the old man stunned with my obviously superior intelligence.

While all these thoughts were whizzing around in my brain, and my heart rate was soaring ever upwards, I realized that my companion was looking at me curiously, obviously waiting for an answer.

'Well,' I began hesitantly, 'it's a sort of ...'

No, that wouldn't do. I tried again.

'You could think of it in terms of ...'

The old man leaned more intently across the table, his spoonful of Weetabix suspended precariously on its way to his mouth.

'I suppose,' I offered as my final attempt, 'it's a kind of ... uh ... communication ... thing.'

Exhausted, I sat back and resumed my meal, trying desperately not to look at what I knew would be the old man's incredulous face.

There was a long silence, during which time we both ruminated over our cereal, and I fervently hoped that he was not going to pursue this to the advanced level.

Eventually, he leaned forward again, and patting me gently on the hand, said,

'I'm sure you're going to find it *very useful* ...'

MORAL

If you know, say, and if you don't know, be honest and say you don't know – and if all else fails, learn how to bluff convincingly!

REFLECTION

Communication
Humour
Self-esteem

50

INTRODUCTION

I wrote this story for someone I knew who had suffered from depression on and off for a number of years. He used to think of himself as Atlas, and said that he sometimes felt as though he were bearing the cares of the whole world on his shoulders. An additional problem in long-term depression is that it can become a way of life, and it becomes impossible for the sufferer to see any other way. I hoped that the story might alleviate some of the weight – for him or for anybody else who might feel the same.

THE TALE

Atlas' Tale

For many years, Atlas had carried the weight of the whole world upon his shoulders. And sometimes he moaned, because the weight of the world was so great, and sometimes he wept, because the cares of those living in the world were so great, and he was sad for them. But Atlas steadfastly did his duty; and in all those years he had never dared to look up, nor stretch his weary back, for in doing so, he might drop his precious charge.

And then one day, a beautiful maiden appeared before Atlas, bearing wine and food, saying, 'Why are you weeping, Atlas? Look up. Put down your burden. Come and drink and eat, and refresh yourself.'

But Atlas said, 'Go hence and do not distract me. For it is my task to carry the weight of the whole world upon my shoulders, and I cannot let it go.'

And then the Devil appeared before Atlas, bearing gold and silver, and other riches beyond compare.

'Why are you weeping, Atlas? Look up. Put down your heavy burden. Come and share these spoils with me.'

But Atlas said, 'Go hence and do not distract me. For it is my task to carry the weight of the whole world upon my shoulders, and I cannot let it go.'

And then Zeus, Father of all the gods appeared before Atlas, and said, 'My son, I am well pleased with your work. For a thousand years you have borne the weight of the whole world upon your shoulders. And now it is time for you to be released from this wearisome burden. Look up, Atlas.

Look up and know I love you.'

And Atlas looked up and saw his father, Zeus, smiling and beckoning him with open arms.

And Zeus said, 'Stand up, Atlas, stand up straight and tall, and let the strength and the power return to your body.'

And as Atlas stood up, and straightened his mighty body, the world, which had been planted so firmly and for so long on his broad shoulders, floated slowly upwards into the heavens.

And Zeus said, 'Behold the world my son. You have filled the world with so much of your strength and your power and your love that it can now support itself. See how it rises up into the heavens. The world need not be a burden to you any longer.'

But Atlas wept and said, 'But what shall become of me, Master? I have carried the world for so long, and if I have no world, what am I to do? What shall be my purpose?'

And Zeus embraced him and said, 'You have toiled long enough, Atlas. Now it is time for you to sit at my right hand, and enjoy food and wine and all manner of riches that you so rightly deserve. And your purpose, together with mine, will be to watch over not just the world, but all the planets in the galaxy.'

And Atlas stepped up and took his place beside Zeus, and as he did so he looked out far into the galaxy, and saw beautiful moons and suns and shooting stars, and at the same time he heard the sounds of song and music and laughter floating through the air, and his heart was filled with such a joy and peace that he had not felt for a thousand years.

And Zeus embraced him and said, 'Welcome home, my son.'

MORAL

We all need to put down our cares from time to time, look up and see far out into the galaxy.

REFLECTION

Motivation
Re-framing
Inspiration
Dealing with change
Success not failure

References

Bandler, R. and Grinder, J. (1975) *The Structure of Magic*, 1, California Science and Behaviour Books, Palo Alto, CA.

Bettelheim, B. (1991) *The Uses of Enchantment: The Meaning and Importance of Fairy Tales*, Knopf, New York.

Boje, D. M. (1991) 'Consulting and change in the storytelling organisation', *Journal of Organisational Change Management*, 4, 7–17.

Buzan, T. (1993) *The Mind Map Book*, BBC Books, London.

Campbell, J. and Moyers, B. (1988) *The Power of Myth*, Doubleday, New York.

Carnegie, D. (1936) *How to Win Friends and Influence People*, Dale Carnegie & Associates, Inc., New York.

Carroll, L. (1865) *Alice's Adventures in Wonderland*, Penguin, London.

Colwell, E. (1980) *Storytelling*, Bodley Head Ltd., London.

Dilts, R. (1994) *Effective Presentation Skills*, Meta Publications, USA.

Egan, K. (1989) 'Memory, imagination and learning: connected by the story', *Phi-Delta-Kappan*, 70, February, 455–9.

Evans, G. and Evans, R. (1989) 'Cognitive mechanisms in learning from metaphors', *Journal of Experimental Education*, 58, 5–19.

Fowles, J. (1977) *The Magus*, Jonathan Cape, UK.

Gibran, K. (1923) *The Prophet*, Penguin, London.

Grasha, T. (1990) 'The naturalistic approach to learning styles', *College Teaching*, 38, Summer, 106–113.

Handy, C. (1976) *Understanding Organisations*, Penguin Publishing, London.

Hanford, S. A. (1954) *Aesop's Fables*, Penguin Books, London.

Harter, N. and Harter, K. (1993) 'Using *Aesop's Fables* to teach conflict resolution', *Delta Kappa Gamma Bulletin*, 59 (3), 42–6.

Jensen, E. (1988) *Superteaching*, Turning Point Press, California.

Kipling, R. (1987) *Just So Stories*, Pavilion Books, London.

Lakoff, G. and Johnson, M. (1980) *Metaphors we Live By*, University of

Chicago Press.

Lozanov, G. (1979) *Suggestology and Outlines of Suggestopedia*, Gordon and Breach, New York.

Mellon, N. (1992) *Storytelling and the Art of Imagination*, Element Books, Shaftesbury, UK.

Milne, A. A. (1926) *The World of Pooh*, Methuen Children's Books, London.

Nelson, P. 'Autobiography in Five Short Chapters', in Black, C. *Repeat After Me*, Denver MAC, 1985.

Neuhauser, P. (1993) *Corporate Legends and Lore*, McGraw-Hill Inc. New York.

Ortony, A. (ed.) (1993) *Metaphor and Thought*, Cambridge University Press.

Ortony, A. (1975) 'Why metaphors are necessary and not just nice', *Educational Theory*, 25, Winter, 45–53.

Peters, T. and Waterman R. (1982) *In Search of Excellence*, Harper and Row, New York.

Petrie, H. and Oshlag, R. (1993) 'Metaphor and Learning' in Ortony, A. (ed.), *Metaphor and Thought*, Cambridge University Press, 579–98.

Roddick, A. (1992) *Body and Soul*, Ebury Press, London.

Rodenburg, P. (1992) *The Right to Speak*, Methuen Drama, London.

Rosen, B. (1988) *And None of it was Nonsense*, Mary Glasgow Publications Ltd, USA.

Semler, R. (1993) *Maverick!* Random House, London.

Simons, P. R. J. (1984) 'Instructing with analogies', *Journal of Educational Psychology*, 76, 513–27.

Sperry, R. (1964) 'The great commissure', *Scientific American*, January.

Stewart, V. (1990) *The David Solution*, Gower Publishing Company, Aldershot, UK.

Sticht, T. (1993) 'Educational Uses of Metaphor' in Ortony, A. (ed.), *Metaphor and Thought*, Cambridge University Press, 622–7.

Teal, T. (ed.), (1996) *First Person*, Harvard Business School of Publishing, Boston, USA.

Thurber, J. (1940) *'Fables for our Time'*, reprinted by arrangement with Rosemary A. Thurber and the Barbara Thurber Hogenson Agency.

Further reading

Baker, A. and Greene, E. (1977) *Storytelling: Art and Technique*, R. R. Bowker Company, New York.

Bandler, R. and Grinder, J. (1979) *Frogs into Princes*, Real People Press, USA.

Bartoli, J. (1985) 'Metaphor, mind, and meaning: the narrative mind in action', *Language Arts*, 62, 332–42.

Briggs, R. (1972) *The Fairy Tale Treasury*, Puffin Books, London.

Bullough, R. (1994) 'Personal metaphors', *American Educational Research Journal*, 31, Spring, 197–224.

Buzan, T. (1977) *Make the Most of your Mind*, Pan Books Ltd, London.

Canfield, J. and Hansen, M. (1993) *Chicken Soup for the Soul*, Health Communications Inc., Florida, USA.

Cotterell, A. (1986) *World Mythology*, Oxford University Press.

Dryden, G. and Vos, J. (1994) *The Learning Revolution*, Accelerated Learning Systems, Aylesbury, UK.

Gordon, D. (1978) *Therapeutic Metaphors*, Meta Publications, USA.

Gross, R. (1987) *Psychology – the Science of Mind and Behaviour*, Edward Arnold (Publishers) Limited, London.

Kaye, M. (1996) 'Organisational myths and storytelling as communication management', *Journal of the Australian and New Zealand Academy of Management*, 1 (2), 1–11.

Laborde, G. (1983) *Influencing with Integrity*, Syntony, California.

Miller, R. M. (1976) 'The dubious case for metaphors in educational writing', *Educational Theory*, 26, 174–81.

O'Connor, J. and Seymour, J. (1990) *Introducing Neuro-linguistic Programming*, HarperCollins Publishers, London.

Ornstein, R. (1977) *The Psychology of Consciousness*, Jovanovich Inc., USA.

Rodenburg, P. (1993) *The Need for Words*, Methuen Drama, London.

Rosen, E. (1982) *My Voice will go with you*, W. W. Norton, New York.

Sanders, D. (1987) 'Capturing the magic of metaphor', *Learning 87*, 15, 36–9.

Silva, J. and Miele, P. (1978) *The Silva Mind Control Method*, Granada Publishing Limited, London.

Vos Savant, M. (1990) *Brain Power*, Piatkus Publishing, London.

Young, J. (1990) *Programmes of the Brain*, Oxford University Press.

Index